Why Men Don't Ask for Directions
and Other Life Observations

Why Men Don't Ask for Directions
and Other Life Observations

By Roger Dale Loring

BELLE ISLE BOOKS
www.belleislebooks.com

ISBN: 978-0-9859358-8-7
Library of Congress Control Number: 2013931093

Printed in the United States

Published by
BELLE ISLE BOOKS
www.belleislebooks.com

To my wife, Lana, who thirty-seven years ago
was my reason to stop dating.

TABLE OF CONTENTS

To my wife, Lana, who thirty-seven years ago was my reason to stop dating.

TABLE OF CONTENTS

INTRODUCTION

I have finally written a book, but believe me when I tell you that it was not an easy task. Part of the difficulty stemmed from my long-held fascination with the French language. Because of that fascination, I decided to write the first draft in French, even though I don't know any French. Actually, I just wrote words that sort of looked like French, but despite their appearance, they were not French words. This technique created a major problem when writing the second draft because I found it almost impossible to translate sort-of-French-looking words into English.

Another major stumbling block in writing this book was the fact that I didn't have anything significant to say and I'm almost certain that saying significant things can be rather important in writing a book. Actually, I haven't said anything significant since I was in the fifth grade when one day I suggested to Sally Sue Sowers that we should go behind the baseball backstop at recess and play doctor. Even then I was obsessed with French, so I made my suggestion in sort-of-French-sounding words. She didn't understand what I was saying, and neither did I, so my plan never came to fruition, which probably was a good thing. Never having played "doctor," I wasn't sure if I was to be the doctor or the patient.

When I originally decided to write a book, I fully intended to write a five-hundred-page novel. Hopefully it would become the Great American Novel. But then I realized that the chances that my first book would become the Great American Novel were rather small. I then decided to change my plan. If I couldn't write the Great American Novel, I would write the Great Icelandic Novel.

Since I was certain I had not been required in high school to read a novel written by an Icelandic author and my high school English teachers only made their students read the "great" novels, I was confident that the Great Icelandic Novel probably had not yet been written. Perhaps I could do it.

Whether my finished product would be the Great Icelandic Novel or the Great American Novel, I had a terrific idea for the beginning. The first sentence was going to be "It was the best of times; it was the worst of times." After trying that line out on one of my friends, he informed me that those words had already been used by Charles Dickens, and apparently used rather successfully. While I understood that he used the line because it really is pretty catchy, I still thought I could make it better and I intended to work on it.

One of my dreams in writing a novel was that it would be the kind of novel that could eventually be made into a movie starring an important actor like Jackie Chan. I even envisioned being at the Academy Awards to receive an Oscar for my writing. But it was even more exciting to think about walking down the red carpet and having Joan Rivers critique my clothes. That's when you know you have arrived.

The plot for my novel, which I believed had "movie" written all over it, concerned an aging opera singer who, during the intermission of a performance at The Met, watches a program on MTV and sees a rapper perform. Fascinated by the hip-hop style of music, he decides to forego his opera career and instead become a rapper. He immediately departs the theater, leaving half of the audience wondering what will happen to Figaro, and the other half, the husbands who were at the opera to make their wives happy, breathing a sigh of relief thinking that the production would have to be stopped. While husbands know about relief pitchers and back-up quarterbacks, they don't know about understudies.

Anyway, I thought I was making good progress with my idea. I was creating some incredibly devious plot twists and turns, but I began to realize that I was not coming up with enough comedic parts and really cool action sequences to land Chan in the lead role.

The fact of the matter was that I was arriving at the conclusion that writing a novel, whether it be Great American or even Great Icelandic, was really hard. On more than one occasion I was heard to mutter, "Writing a novel is really hard."

I decided to give up on writing a novel. Instead I would write a book of some other kind, the kind that is not a novel. As it turns out, the book I wrote is a book of observations. To be exact, my observations about the human condition and all of the varied aspects of that condition. Now that at least sounds kind of impressive. If my book cannot be a novel that becomes a movie, I will settle for a book that at least sounds kind of impressive. Some of the observations in the book are heartfelt, some are made up, some are silly, and most are meant to be humorous. Some are expressed in poetry and some in prose, but they are all mine.

While my book will no doubt never be made into a movie, maybe, just maybe, it might have promise as a TV sitcom about an opera singer turned rapper who likes to make observations, spoken in sort-of-French-sounding words, about a lot of stuff. Each episode of the series will begin with the opera singer/rapper saying, "It was the top-of-the-line times; it was the bottom-of-the-barrel times." Eat your heart out, Dickens. Now, read on and enjoy.

Megabyte Modem
(Since I didn't use a pen to write this book,
I don't have a pen name, but this is my word processor name.)

Section One – Nuclear Physics

For no apparent reason, I have divided this book into three sections and this is the introduction to the first section. Since you are going to find out anyway, it turns out that the essays in this section have absolutely nothing to do with nuclear physics. In fact, neither the word "nuclear" nor the word "physics" appears in any of the essays that follow. Actually, I don't know a single thing about nuclear physics, or any science for that matter.

I chose "nuclear physics" as the title for this section because it gives the book a certain air of intelligence, which without the Section One title would not be readily apparent in any part of the book. The fact of the matter is that the essays in this section actually deal with a bunch of nonscientific topics about which I also know very little.

A Close Encounter of the Meaningful Kind

I met him by accident. We bumped into each other as we both attempted to purchase a newspaper from a machine outside of a drugstore. Apologizing, he stepped back to let me deposit my money first. When I opened the machine, there was only one copy left. Feeling a bit guilty because he had been so polite, I offered to let him have the paper.

"No, that's okay," he said, "I'll just go inside the store and get one."

I knew he wouldn't be able to do that. "I'm afraid they don't sell this newspaper inside. Here, take this one. I'll go buy another paper. They're all about the same."

He rebuffed my offer. "No, you keep the paper. It really doesn't make any difference to me either. I'll probably be mentioned in most of the newspapers anyway."

My curiosity was suddenly piqued by this strange response. "What if there aren't any newspapers left inside?" My question was asked in an attempt to buy time while I quickly tried to think of a way to discover the identity of this now intriguing stranger.

"I really don't need a newspaper," he said. "I'll just get some coffee at the lunch counter and listen to what people are saying about me."

My piqued curiosity was now peaking. I gazed intently at the man, trying so very hard to place his face. Obviously he had to be someone important, or at the very least, famous. I didn't know anyone from either category. My first thought was to ask him if he was SOMEBODY, but I realized that question would be a bit tacky. I opted for a more subtle approach, one that would continue my buying-more-time ploy.

"Well, I've got a few minutes," I said. "Let's both go get some coffee and we can share the paper. You can have whatever section you think you will be mentioned in and I'll just read another section."

"Oh, I imagine there is something about me in all of the sections."

Now my curiosity was being pushed to the limit. I had to know this guy's identity. Why would so many people be talking and writing about him? Was he an actor whom I just didn't recognize because he was disguised as the nondescript little man wearing thick glasses who now stood before me? Maybe he was a powerful politician whom I didn't recognize because he preferred working behind the scenes instead of appearing on Sunday morning talk shows? Perhaps he was a former guest on one of those afternoon programs that feature ex-lovers, potential lovers, or multiple lovers, all of whom are related in some way. Anyway, I decided to ditch the subtle approach.

"Excuse me, I'm rather embarrassed to ask this question, and I don't mean to be nosy, but should I know you? What is your name?"

He just smiled. "I don't exactly have a name."

That clearly was not a satisfactory answer. It just added to the mystery and to my frustration. I wasn't sure if he was being evasive, or whether he was being a wise guy because he felt I was prying, which I was. In either case, I wasn't about to let it drop now. My curiosity was turning to annoyance.

"No name, huh? Well, I guess you don't have a problem with junk mail." I was making a weak attempt at humor to keep myself from grabbing this guy by his scrawny little neck and choking him until he told me who in the heck he was!

He just smiled again. I didn't want smiles, I wanted a name. I decided to become bolder in my questioning, but grabbing him by his neck was still a viable option.

"What is on your paychecks, since you don't have a name?"

3

"Paychecks? Oh, I don't work. Well, I suppose that's not exactly true. I do have a job of sorts, but I don't get paid."

"Yeah, well maybe you don't get paid because no one knows who you are! Why would you work at a job that doesn't pay anyway? Are you rich?"

"No, I'm not rich. The fact of the matter is that I don't get paid because what I do is really quite easy. You see, my job is simply to go around saying things."

I suspected he could tell by the expression on my face that I was terribly confused by his answer. In fact, I was dumbfounded.

He confirmed my suspicion. "I can tell by the expression on your face that you are terribly confused, perhaps even dumbfounded. Actually, everyone reacts that way. Maybe I should clear things up by introducing myself. I am one of *they*."

That bit of information did nothing to clear up anything. I had wanted an introduction a long time ago, but now that I had it, it made absolutely no sense. I eyed his neck and took one step closer. "*They*, huh. Well, I'm sorry, but I still don't understand."

He seemed a bit hurt by my lack of understanding. And for one brief moment, as I stared at this little man who now had a sad expression on his face, I felt a bit guilty about wanting to get physical with him. I stepped back, willing to hear more explanation, but I still kept his neck within my line of sight.

He gave me a quizzical look as he continued. "Surely you've heard of *they*? Think about it. Haven't you heard someone comment as to how *they* said this, or *they* said that? Well, I'm one of the *they*."

Well, you could have knocked me over with a helium balloon. At last, he was actually beginning to make some sense. "Wait a minute, let me get this straight. Yesterday some guy told me *they* say if you rub garlic on your head, hair will grow. And last week someone told me that *they* say the economy will rebound soon. Are you telling me you are one of the people who go around saying those things?"

"Exactly. In fact, I'm the one who made that comment about the economy."

"You know about economics, do you?"

"Oh, heck no. I can't even balance my checkbook. But that's the beauty of being one of *they*. I can say anything I want, despite what I may or may not know about the subject in question. Knowledge isn't important. My job is simply to give the media something to use for their stories and people gathered around the water cooler at work something to talk about. Shucks, because of me, folks can argue, discuss, debate, or whatever, without being burdened by facts. Instead, people can just attribute their information to *they*, an attribution that seemingly carries the weight of numbers. It keeps a free flow of discussion going without being slowed by burdensome details. Who has time for details anyway? And surely you know free discussion is essential to our democracy, which means I have a tremendous responsibility in my job."

I was stunned, but somewhat satisfied. "Well I'll be a son-of-a-gun. I've always wondered who *they* were. It's truly an honor to meet you. Are there a lot of other *they* out there, or do you have to do it all?"

"Actually, there are legions of us at several different levels. I'm at a lower level right now, but I certainly aspire to move up to the top one day."

My puzzlement was starting to return. "Different levels? Move up?"

"Well, at present, I am just one of *they*. There's not much prestige with simply being one of *they*. Ah, but someday I plan on being an *unnamed source*, or *someone unauthorized to speak on this subject*. If I work hard, I might even be able to become *a senior administration official*. These labels would allow me to make statements that would be quoted in *The New York Times* or *The Washington Post*, instead of *The National Enquirer* and local newspapers. I can dare to dream."

It was truly an amazing encounter, but it had to come to an end. We both had some place to go, so we parted company. I headed off to work and he went inside the drugstore, no doubt to spread more information. In fact, as I was leaving, I heard him say to someone, "Hey, did you know that they say a person's IQ can be increased by twenty points if they eat asparagus and peanut butter on wheat bread?"

I shook my head and smiled. How gullible we can be when we think if *they* say it, it must be true. Then I remembered I needed to go to the store after work. I was low on peanut butter and asparagus.

I Think I Know What I Think

Recently I thought it would be nice if my wife and I went out to see a movie, something we rarely do. The fact that we don't go to movie theaters very often is because of me. If I am going to watch a movie, I'd much rather do it at home for a variety of reasons.

First of all, my taste in movies is actually quite simple and I can almost always find something on TV that suits me. You see, I prefer old movies. By "old," I mean anything made before 1964, the year I graduated from high school, and pretty much the last time I went out to see a movie.

Besides being able to see the types of movies I prefer, another very important reason why I like staying home is because it is much cheaper than attending a theater. Granted, the cost of admission to a theater really isn't too terrible, but if I choose to get popcorn and sodas for my wife and me, the cost is greater than my monthly mortgage payment. The bank failures over the past year or so were not because of risky loans to people trying to buy houses, but instead, the foolish loans made to folks trying to feed themselves at a movie theater.

Anyway, throwing caution and my checkbook to the wind, I asked my wife if she wanted to go out to see a movie. Her response clearly indicated the rarity of such an action on my part. "That would be great. I hear they have talkies now."

Her sarcasm aside, I was determined to go out to see this movie. It starred a guy I had seen on a talk show. He was hawking the movie and he seemed nice enough. I had never seen him in a movie, except for the thirty-second clip that was shown on the talk show, but I was willing to take a chance. Sometimes I am just a wild and crazy guy, about every forty or forty-five years to be exact.

Perhaps more important than liking the actor when he exchanged quips with the talk show host was the fact that I was drawn to the movie because it was supposed to be a comedy. Since day after day I read the newspapers and watch the news on TV, I definitely needed some laughs, knee-slapping, big-belly, bring-tears-to-your-eyes laughs. I was certain this movie, albeit a "new" movie, would still fill the bill. It wasn't *The Three Stooges*, but I was willing to take a chance.

Fortunately, our night at the movies was enjoyable in almost every way, with one exception being my inability to find a low interest loan for popcorn and sodas. Nevertheless, I did thoroughly enjoy the movie itself. I loved the plot, the acting, and I was certain the cinematographer on this movie had also done an excellent job, even though I didn't have the slightest idea as to what cinematographers do. When I left the theater, although now deeply in debt, I was as happy as a squirrel standing at the base of an oak tree.

Then my acorns vanished. The very next day I happened to read a review of the movie. I was crushed, suddenly full of doubts, questioning my ability to know good from bad. You see, the reviewer, some guy who is paid to watch movies, hated the movie. He didn't have one complimentary thing to say about it. Nada. Nothing. Nil. He even panned the cinematographer. Being a professional, he obviously knew exactly what cinematographers are supposed to do and, therefore, what this cinematographer didn't do.

Well, as you can imagine, I felt terrible. I was embarrassed. I had recommended the movie to several of my friends. I was afraid that if they read the review they would think of me as some sort of movie charlatan, which at the moment I felt like I was. I was sure these friends would never again take my advice about movies. If a discussion about a movie would ever come up in my presence, I was sure they would whisper among themselves, "Don't ask Roger about the movie, he clearly has terrible taste in films." I wanted to call all of them and explain I was just kidding in my praise of such an obviously horrible film. Then I could say, "You've been punked!"

I really began to feel depressed about the entire matter. After all, it was a shock to my emotional stability to learn what I thought was really good was in fact a bomb. It was a bomb because a professional movie critic had said so. It was in black and white for the whole world to read. It definitely was a blow to my ego to realize that I didn't even know a bad movie when I saw one.

As I contemplated this point, I began to panic. It suddenly struck me that if I didn't know how to judge movies, then maybe I didn't know how to judge anything. Maybe the steak and shrimp I had so thoroughly enjoyed at my favorite restaurant last week was actually terrible. And maybe that restaurant was in reality just a greasy spoon. Every decision I had made in my entire life was now suspect.

I decided to go see my friend Waldo. I call him Waldo the Wino. Actually, I don't know if he drinks wine or not. I don't have any idea what is in the bottle he always keeps in a brown paper bag at his side. But I do know that whatever it is, he drinks out of it a lot. Regardless of what Waldo drinks or doesn't drink, he still can usually cheer me up when I feel exactly as I was feeling then. Even though he can be a bit insulting, he actually is a pretty neat old guy. And he knows stuff.

When I arrived, he was sitting in his favorite chair clutching the aforementioned brown paper bag. "Waldo, old buddy, I'm having an emotional and intellectual crisis. My life is a shambles and I'm a nervous wreck. I'm a failure. I'm confused. I need your help. You've got to tell me what to do."

Waldo looked straight into my eyes, took a drink, and calmly said, "You really are a sniveling idiot. Sit down and shut up!"

His words were like a slap across my face. Thanking him because I needed that, I quickly explained the whole situation to him. I told him how reading that movie review had precipitated my downward spiral to my present unstable position.

He shook his head and took a big drink from the mysterious bottle in the brown paper bag. Sitting back in his chair, he began to speak. "Listen, melon head, you're about as foolish as old Jasper Plank back in my hometown. One day he decided to see the world. Guess he didn't have a good enough view from his place. Anyway, he set out on his journey, but he never got past the edge of town. There was a railroad crossing there and when old Jasper got to the crossing, he looked up and saw the sign. It simply said, 'Stop, Look, and Listen.' So, he stopped, he looked, and he listened. Day after day, he stayed stopped and he continued to look and listen."

I wasn't sure where the story was going. "So what happened?"

"Not much of anything until winter came. That's when old Jasper froze to death. It was the blizzard of '57, I believe."

My jaw dropped. "Waldo, what does this story mean? What does poor Jasper Plank's untimely, and rather weird, demise have to do with me?"

"It's simple, dome head, Jasper passed on because he suffered from the affliction you now have. He believed everything he read. He believed that if someone wrote something that got printed for anyone to read, they must know more than he did. The point is that he let a sign keep him from his quest and you are letting some review in the newspaper keep you from enjoying life. If one man's opinion about a movie can put you in such a state, I suggest you stop reading movie reviews. And then maybe you will leave me alone."

"You know, Waldo, what you say does make sense. I don't need some movie critic to tell me what I should or shouldn't like. I'm my own man. I have my own opinions. I do have good judgment. I know what I like and I don't care if anyone else likes it or not. Thank you, old buddy, thank you very much. I really do feel much better. I have my confidence back again."

I did indeed feel better and I couldn't wait to get back home. And what the heck, I was going to ask my wife if she wanted to go see another movie. And after seeing the movie, I would call all of my friends and give them my opinion, my very valid opinion, about the relative merits of what I had seen.

As I headed out to my car, Waldo yelled out to me. "By the way, bald boy, I saw that movie too. It stunk!"

On second thought, maybe my wife and I would just stay home and watch an old movie on TV, and after she went to bed, I'd tell the dog whether or not the movie was any good.

I'm Sorry, Are You Talking to Me?

This is the age of the cell phone, and because of this apparently useful little device, people are now talking more than ever. Wherever you look, there are people talking on cell phones. They talk while they are backing out of their driveways, standing in line at grocery stores, watching movies, walking down streets, delivering babies, baking sweet potato pies, and the list goes on forever. It is quite obvious that talking on cell phones is the thing to do.

Despite the increased amount of talking that is taking place, I maintain that conversation is still becoming a lost art. I realize this seems to be a rather large paradox, but nevertheless, that is exactly what is happening. While there are indeed large numbers of people talking and talking and then talking some more, real conversation is not taking place. There is not a verbal exchange of ideas. People are talking, but no one is communicating.

The reason for the lack of communication nowadays is because even though people are talking a lot, with or without those beloved cell phones, no one is listening. Everyone has something to say, but after they say it, they quickly want to say something else. Responses to what they say really are not necessary. In fact, responses just seem to get in the way. You see, conversations today are actually monologues. Only one person is actually participating.

Evidently many people are so preoccupied with their own lives, they don't even have a passing interest in anything else. So, when talking to such people, you may notice that they smile, ask questions and pretend to be concerned about what is being said, but it is all a guise. The fact of the matter is that absolutely no attention is being

Gratitude ★ Blessings ★ Happiness

Gratitude ★ Blessings ★ Friendship ★ Happiness

paid to what is being said to them, and the questions they ask only provide a break in the action so they can think about what they will say next. I'm of the belief that one could talk utter nonsense to such people and they would never notice. Actually, I tried such an approach the other day when I encountered someone I hadn't seen for quite some time....

Me: Hey, Ralph, long time no see.

Ralph: Hello, Rog, how have you been?

Me: Not so good. When I was taking a shower this morning, all of the fingers on my left hand fell off. I hate when that happens.

Ralph: That's great. For myself, things aren't so good. First of all, I've been fighting a cold for weeks along with terrible migraines. But I've got way too much to do to let that slow me down. How's Lana?

Me: Wow, funny thing about Lana. Lately she has really started to grow. We measured her this morning and she is almost eight feet tall now. We are pretty sure the Lakers are going to offer her a contract next week. She'll probably turn them down because she wants to be a shooting guard instead of a center. How's Sally?

Ralph: I'm glad to hear Lana is doing well. Sally is fine, but she does stay busy. Right now the PTA takes most of her time. She basically runs our PTA. Actually, she pretty much runs every group she's in. Say, speaking of the PTA, are you still a teacher?

Me: No, I quit teaching recently when I was elected President of the United States of America. I miss kids though, so I plan to visit both houses of Congress a lot. The members there act just like the kids I used to teach.

Ralph: I'm sure the kids miss you, too. As usual, I'm busy, busy, busy. I've been putting in a ton of overtime lately. They just can't seem to function at the office if I'm not there. I can't tell you the last time I've been able to kick back and watch a football game on TV. By the way, who's going to the Super Bowl this year?

Me: What? Didn't you hear, they are going to cancel the Super Bowl this year because no one seems to care anymore. On Super Bowl Sunday, instead of a football game there is going to be a tag team mud-wrestling match between Sarah Palin and Tina Fey against Hillary Clinton and Amy Poehler. How cool is that?

Ralph: Shucks, I was hoping the Redskins might have a chance. I sure do envy you for having time to watch football. You always could manage your free time better than me. My problem is that I don't really have any free time. Did I tell you I built a deck on the back of the house, put a new transmission in my car, and painted the guest bedroom while helping my son become an Eagle Scout? I've been busy.

Me: Well, I've been doing a little woodwork and car work myself. I just built a garage out of toothpicks that is an exact replica of the Taj Mahal and I souped up a Model T Ford and won the Daytona 500 while driving backwards. I had to wreck Jimmy Johnson on the last lap to win, but that's just the way I roll.

Ralph: That's nice. My problem is that I'm under so much pressure at work. I have so many important decisions to make every single day. My job has a tremendous amount of responsibility. The bottom line is that I do what I have to do. I wouldn't be where I am today if I couldn't stand the heat in the kitchen.

Me: Pressure? Responsibility? Heat? Man, that's what I felt when I pitched a no-hitter in the seventh game of the World Series last year. And then the very next day I devised a plan to pay off the national debt by the end of next month.

Ralph: That's great. Say, look, it's been great seeing you, but I have to get to work. The boss is coming in today and I have to be there. I'm pretty sure I will get a big promotion today. Take care and I hope to see you soon.

Well, there you have it. Ralph and I talked, but we sure didn't communicate. I'd like to believe Ralph and all of the Ralphs of the world have a hearing problem, but I know better. The problem is that people just don't listen anymore. Hello? I said, people just don't listen anymore!

I'm Making a List and Checking It Twice

I am a list maker. Yes, that's right, I am one of THOSE people. In fact, when one looks at people who make lists, I am right at the top of the list, a position that perhaps only a list maker can fully appreciate. Before my feet hit the floor in the morning, I am reaching for my list, which was made the night before, to see what is in store for me the rest of the day.

While most people need a cup of coffee or a piece of toast or a Bloody Mary before they attempt to greet the new day, I just need to look at my list. Then, and only then, will I know if I am to have a cup of coffee or piece of toast or Bloody Mary before I greet the new day.

My list is important for several reasons. It is my security blanket. It is the set of directions that allows me to function. My ever-present list of things to do is my road map on the often-perilous journey through life. By making a list, I am in effect creating the blueprint for my very existence.

As grandiose as the importance of my having a list may seem to be, I realize that some people who make lists do so for rather mundane reasons, such as having difficulty in remembering things. As these people get older and the memory begins to fade a bit, the list making begins. For myself, my memory is still razor-sharp. And besides that, my memory is razor-sharp. Okay, maybe my memory isn't what it used to be. But if the truth be known, my memory never did amount to much. At least I think that was the way it was.

Actually, I saw the importance of making lists long before I reached the stage where I was sitting in my car and asking myself, did I just get here or am I leaving? I always hoped I had just arrived, because if I was leaving, I didn't know where I was going.

Anyway, I guess one reason why I make lists, other than having a tiny bit of a memory problem, is because at the end of the day, the list in effect represents a kind of certificate of accomplishment. It is tremendously satisfying to see a paper full of crossed-out items that represent a day full of achievement. To be able to draw lines through activities on the list that have been achieved, such as get dressed, take the cap off of the shaving cream, tie shoes, well, how do you adequately describe total serenity?

By the way, I have, as I suspect all list makers have, on occasion accomplished something during the day that was not on my list. Not one to let any feat go unrecognized, I proceed to put the item on my list and then cross it off with a bright red line. In fact, one of the items that is always on my list is the reminder, "If you accomplish something today that is not on this list, add it, and then cross it off with a bright red line."

When I do make my lists, nothing is too important or too trivial to be included. Items might range from "water the flowers" to "clean the garage" to "win the Masters." That last item, "win the Masters," illustrates one of the beauties of my list making. While my lists provide daily supervision for the more humdrum activities I have to face, they also allow me to dream—perhaps "fantasize" is a better word, thus the item, "win the Masters." The point is that list makers don't just focus on today. We don't simply live in the moment. We are indeed aware of the future.

By keeping day-to-day lists of my activities, I am in effect keeping a kind of shorthand diary. Think of how interesting and satisfying it will be for me to take out one of my old lists and see that on June 4, 1991, I cut the grass, found a missing sock after a planned effort to search every area where socks might hide, and had a cup of coffee, piece of toast, and Bloody Mary for breakfast. Imagine how impressed people will be when I am able to relate in detail the things I accomplished years ago. Okay, maybe no one will care, but the lists will be helpful if I ever write my autobiography. In fact, excuse me a minute while I put that on my list.

Despite the obvious merit of my list making, my wife still finds my obsession with the process to be rather excessive. She is of the opinion that by making lists and then following them so diligently, I become too organized, too much like a computerized robot. She feels my dependence on lists destroys spontaneity…a sense of fun…a sense of excitement…a sense of daring.

My wife's attitude is that if she wakes up some morning and feels moved to rearrange every piece of furniture in the house, then go for it. If she feels like we should take an unplanned trip to, say, Secaucus, New Jersey, then do it. By the way, does anyone take a trip to Secaucus, planned or unplanned? Anyway, the point is that she definitely is a spur-of-the-moment, let-it-all-hang-out, do-something-different kind of person. She is just the kind of person that can make a list maker sweat and break out in hives.

Well, in order to avoid such an unfortunate situation and to dispel any negative perceptions my wife might have about my desire to know what I am going to do before I do it, I plan to demonstrate once and for all that I am not a computerized robot. In fact, my list for tomorrow proves it. On that list she will see, big and bold, item number seventeen: "be spontaneous!" That should remove any doubts about my being too rigid, too set in my ways. I think that item on my list clearly illustrates that I am definitely a wild and crazy guy! In fact, I think I'll call a motel in Secaucus right now and book a room for sometime next month. According to my list, I should have some free time by then.

Do I Look Like a Member of a NASCAR Pit Crew?

As a rule, I am not easily impressed or intimidated. If I should find myself in the presence of a powerful or famous person, I do not become nervous or awestruck. I do not see any difference in meeting a United States senator, movie star, or grocery store bag boy. Talking to a Super Bowl-winning quarterback would be like talking to a mailman. I'm no more impressed by Bill the brain surgeon than by Willie the window washer.

But despite my usual laid-back attitude, I must confess there is one type of person that can shatter my "oh-so-cool" exterior. If I meet someone who introduces himself by saying, "Hello, I'm Joe the auto mechanic," well, all bets are off. I become a lump of lime Jell-O. My IQ, which is already dangerously low, drops fifty points and I become a babbling idiot.

The inferiority complex that surfaces when I am around people who spend their time working on cars clearly stems from my limited, no, make that nonexistent, knowledge about mechanical things, particularly Henry Ford's brainchild. As a male, I realize that I am not supposed to admit that I don't know about tools and cars, but after meeting me, it becomes rather obvious that I am indeed mechanically challenged. Heck, for a long time I thought ball-peen hammer and claw hammer were brothers of the rap singer M.C. Hammer.

My total lack of knowledge about cars in particular goes back to my high school years. As a teenager, while my buddies were changing the oil in their cars, I was struggling to find out how to just check the oil in my car. I certainly couldn't participate in the oil-changing process when I couldn't even determine if I had any oil to change in the first place. And while my friends were able to work on the engines of their cars in order to make them go faster, I was trying to figure out how to put gas in my car so it would go at any speed.

Since I do not have much of a background in tinkering with cars, the workings of an automobile are a deep, dark mystery to me; but then again, so is a flashlight. But I don't want to give the impression that I am totally ignorant about all things dealing with a car. To be exact, I can lock the doors, roll the windows up AND down, and use the turn signal, all of which are mechanical devices and yet I have conquered their complexities. So I do feel there is hope for me. In fact, if my wife assembles the jack for me, I can also change a tire. Well, I can at least help her change a tire.

Because of my mechanical shortcomings, I have rather basic expectations for my car. I want it to start when I turn the key, go when I step on the gas, and stop when I apply the brakes. From that point on, I don't much care about all of the many other frills and accessories that cars seem to have today. I'm so old school about technological things, I just want to make calls on my cell phone, no picture taking or texting or connecting to the Internet. I do not want a smartphone. I'm not smart enough.

Now, while my expectations for a car are basic, if any of the required functions fail to work properly, then I sink into what can best be described as a totally clueless state. Unfortunately, I remain in that state when I go to see a mechanic about the car's problem, and what ensues is not a pretty picture.

The problem, as was so dramatically stated in the movie *Cool Hand Luke*—"What we have here is a failure to communicate!"— makes the chances of my car being repaired most difficult. The mechanic doesn't understand me when I explain that the *gizmo* and the *thingamagig* in my engine don't seem to be working properly. And I definitely don't understand him when he throws out such terms as distributor and piston. As far as I'm concerned, the former sells beer, and I suppose they sell other things, but beer comes to mind, and the latter is a professional basketball player in Detroit.

The entire process is terribly frustrating and embarrassing, but not near as frustrating and embarrassing as when I have to go to an auto parts store to purchase a necessary part for my car. I had always assumed that simply knowing the name of the part would be sufficient to acquire said part. Evidently the depths of my ignorance about cars knows no bounds.

The procedure to obtain a part turns out to be far too complicated for me. It seems the auto parts dealer needs more information than just the name of a part. And in order to get that information, I am asked what I consider to be rather silly questions, questions, by the way, which I rarely can answer.

When I'm asked what kind of car I have, why can't he just accept my standard answer: "I have a red Chevy"? So what if I don't know the model or year of my car? Is that a felony or something? Don't these auto parts people know that I already have a wealth of information to remember: zip code, social security number, phone number (regular and cell), credit card number, and street address? Is all of the information I'm asked to provide about my car all that necessary anyway?

As it turns out, it is. And in fact, sometimes even more specific information is essential. For example, I remember once being asked the number of cylinders my car had. Okay, so I didn't know that information, but if it was so doggone important, then the car manufacturers should put it in some conspicuous place in the car, like the center of the windshield.

It's as if these auto mechanics and auto parts dealers think I am a driver for NASCAR or something. Hey, I've never wanted to drive for NASCAR. Well, maybe I have had a fantasy about that, but I definitely have never wanted to be a pit crew member. They have to know way too much stuff. I bet they all own smartphones.

Why Men Don't Ask for Directions

My wife and I do a fair amount of traveling and, more often than not, we travel by car. We enjoy our trips and, for the most part, they run smoothly. But there are those occasions when, during the course of our journey, we get lost. I say "we," but in reality, it is possible that I am the one who usually is responsible for us losing our way.

Actually, I am of the opinion that it really doesn't matter how we get lost, the dilemma is what to do when we get lost. For myself, I feel that I can eventually find the way by driving around for a while until, poof, the correct road magically appears. In point of fact, my technique is a bit like the hunt-and-peck method of typing. If I hunt and peck enough I can eventually type a word and if I type enough words, I eventually have a sentence.

My wife doesn't so much believe in magic. She also types without ever looking at the keys. Consequently, she doesn't put much stock in my method for finding the way after becoming lost. She puts her trust in common sense, which to her means stopping and asking for directions.

The difference of opinions about which plan is better in solving the "where-in-the-heck-are-we" quandary has yet to be resolved. Until now. Recently I was having a discussion with a buddy about the disagreement between wives and husbands in finding a solution to the "we're lost" problem. He related a story to me about how on his last trip with his wife, they got lost. After driving around for a while looking for the "magical" correct road to appear, his wife tried to convince him to stop and ask for directions. He finally yielded to her persistent pleas and pulled into a gas station in the middle of nowhere. The story went like this....

"Excuse me, but I'm lost and I'm not sure how that happened. I was following all of the road signs, but suddenly there weren't any signs. Could you tell me how to get to Fulton's Grove?"

The young man who was pumping gas into an old truck seemed a bit puzzled by the question. He thought for a moment and then a smile crossed his face.

"Fulton's Grove, huh. Yep, I can help you with that one. I've never been there, but my grandpa used to run moonshine over that way and I heard him tell stories a million times about his trips there. Heck, I think I could get there with my eyes shut."

"Well, I plan to keep my eyes open and I sure would appreciate it if you could give me the directions."

"No problem. First of all, go back down the road 'bout eight miles or so. You'll see the Jackson farm on the right." Before my friend could protest that he didn't know the Jacksons or what their farm looked like, the young man rapidly continued on with his directions.

"Across from the farm on the left is a dirt road. When Grandpa was running shine, it was a really nice road, but it ain't much now. It's all grown up with weeds, so look closely or you won't even see it. Probably the best way to find it is to look right across from Lucy Mae Jackson's bedroom window and you'll see the road. That Lucy Mae is a looker and she never pulls her shades down at night. Anyway, once you get on the road, go 'bout a mile or two till you come to a fork in the road."

At this point, the young man finished pumping the gas and started to go inside to pay.

"Hey, excuse me, but do I turn left or right at the fork in the road?"

"What? Right or left? No, mister, you go straight. My grandpa stuck that fork in the road to mark a good spot to hide the shine if the sheriff was getting too close."

"Oh, you literally meant a fork 'in' the road."

"What did you think I meant? Say, you aren't from around here, are you, mister?"

"No, I'm not, that's probably why I'm lost. Could you just go on with the directions please?"

"Okay, but try to pay a little better attention. Just keep going down the road and you'll come to what you'll probably think is the end of the road cause you'll see a big ditch in front of you. Well, it ain't the end. If you drive very carefully, you can get across that ditch. They say when Grandpa got to that ditch, he'd be a'goin' so fast, you know the sheriff would be chasin' him, that he'd clear that ditch in the air. That's where he'd always get away 'cause the sheriff was a'scared to try and clear that ditch in the air."

"What do I do after I get across the ditch?"

"Well, now here's the good part. Once you're on the other side of the ditch, go about a mile and you'll see a big old apple tree on the left. Them apples are the best tastin' apples you'll ever eat. You got to stop and get one, but don't let Bubba Coot see you or he'll probably shoot at you."

"Why is this the good part?"

"Cause them apples are great and Bubba Coot can't shoot a lick. After getting the apples, you'll notice a road behind the tree. It's really more like a path, but I think your car will fit on it."

At this point, my friend interrupted. He tactfully tried to point out that since he wasn't running from the sheriff, he'd prefer a more direct route to Fulton's Grove. The young man did seem a bit hurt that his grandpa's legendary moonshine route wasn't acceptable. He said he didn't know any other way, but that Orville the mechanic might know how to get there. He then jumped into his truck and drove off.

My friend went inside to find Orville, which he did, and he then found himself trying to decipher another set of directions. "Fulton's Grove? Why sure, mister, that's easy to get to. Just go up the road till you come to Route 630 South, or maybe it's 633 South. Anyway, turn left when you get there and go five, or maybe it's ten miles. You'll come to an intersection. Turn right, I'm pretty sure it's a right, and head down the road till you get to Route 1250 or 1050, or something like that. Turn left and go straight ahead till you come to a fork in the road."

"Another fork, huh. Will it be a salad fork or a dinner fork?"

"What? Don't you know a fork in the road is when the road divides? You're not from around here, are you, mister?"

"I was just, I mean, I thought you were, it's just that the young.... Oh, never mind. Do I take the right or left fork?"

"Take the left and go a fer piece and then you'll be at Fulton's Grove, or at least you'll be darn close, if I got all of those turns right."

My friend thanked Orville, got in the car, stared real hard at his wife, and drove off. After driving around for a couple of hours, it became apparent that the turns and route numbers were not correct. During the tour of the countryside, my friend got more directions from a hitchhiker, a waitress, two farmers, and a deputy sheriff. The deputy knew the moonshine route, but he couldn't explain it any better than the young man at the gas station.

Finally my friend got to a place he was familiar with—the gas station where he started. He went to find Orville, but before he got to the garage, he encountered an old man sitting in a rocking chair while whittling on a piece of wood.

"I knew you'd be back. That kid and Orville don't know nothing. If they were standing side by side, they couldn't find each other."

My friend was surprised that the man knew of his plight. But he was also happy that perhaps he had at last found someone who could help him.

"Well, maybe I didn't understand their directions. I don't suppose you could help me?"

"If you woulda asked ask me in the first place, I could have saved you a lot of trouble."

"I guess I didn't see you sitting here. I don't want to make the same mistake twice, so I'm asking now. How do you get to Fulton's Grove?"

The old man sat back in his chair, put down his knife, and looked my friend straight in the eye. "Shucks, mister, any fool knows that you can't get there from here!"

To all women in the world who think asking directions when lost is the way to go, I rest my case. You just can't trust strangers. It's far better to keep driving around, because, poof, the right road will magically appear sooner or later.

My Life in B Flat

While I am mostly satisfied with my life up to this point, that point being the time when I am receiving more and more mail telling me I should soon select some form of Medicare coverage, I do have one great regret in my life. That regret is that I never became accomplished in any musical field. While I do sing in the shower with unbridled enthusiasm, rarely do I sing on key, something I would not be aware of if my wife hadn't pointed it out to me. Consequently, I am never asked to sing at parties. Actually I don't get invitations to parties for any reason. If for some inexplicable reason I would receive an invitation, when people began singing, I would be sent to the store to get some more beer and snacks.

Besides my lack of singing ability, I also cannot play a musical instrument, in or out of the shower. While I had opportunities to learn to play an instrument, I just didn't take advantage of them, hence my one great regret in life.

Like many youngsters, my first contact with the world of music came when my parents signed me up for piano lessons. It was at that time that I wondered what I had done to make them so angry. If I had done something so terribly wrong as to warrant a punishment that consisted of me being subjected to piano lessons from the overly stern Mrs. Meanlady, why didn't my parents simply spank me and send me up to my room without food for several years? That punishment would have shown much more compassion.

Besides the presence of Mrs. Meanlady, the piano lessons were so dreadful to me because I was expected to practice scales and three-note songs for hours at a time. Trust me, I was not interested in practicing scales and three-note songs for hours at a time. I wanted to be catching grasshoppers, learning to ride my bike, or playing baseball in the park. I clearly was not interested in learning to tickle the ivories, although I must confess that I was reaching an age when tickling Angela Fanelli held a budding fascination.

After I pounded my way through only six piano lessons, and yes, pounded is the correct term, I was more than ready to throw in the towel. And after my parents had suffered through five weeks of my practice sessions during which I tried to perfect my pounding techniques, my parents were ready to hand me the towel to throw. Actually, in their case, allowing my escape from Mrs. Meanlady was more of a monetary decision. They decided the money they were spending on my lessons would be better spent buying swamp land in Florida.

My next foray into the world of music occurred several years later when I was introduced to the saxophone in the school band. Playing in the band was a choice my parents made for me, a decision that clearly illustrated that they had either forgotten my disastrous bout with the piano, or they had remembered, and they decided I needed further punishment. Evidently they thought I would be more successful with the saxophone.

Even though my parents made the decision that I would play in the band, I was at least allowed to pick the instrument I wanted to play. The saxophone was my choice because when the band instructor played it, he produced some really cool sounds. As it turned out, I had a love/hate relationship with the saxophone—I loved the idea of playing an instrument that made such really cool sounds, but I hated the fact that I couldn't produce those sounds. To my parents and the band instructor, my frustration could be ended if I would only spend more time practicing.

Their solution to my problem was not what I wanted to hear, but despite my aversion to practicing, I did somehow manage to endure for several more years. In fact, every once in a while I was able to blow into my sax in such a way that it did indeed make a really cool sound. It was enough to keep me going because I thought that just perhaps there would be a time when I could produce that really cool sound more than once a month.

But as I grew older, my interests began to change and producing cool sounds on the saxophone dropped lower and lower on my list of priorities. Finally, at the start of my sophomore year in high school, I realized it was time to end my troublesome relationship with the saxophone. I made my fateful decision to give it up, thereby ending my formal relationship with music.

At the time, my decision to quit playing the sax, or I should say, attempting to play the sax, made a great deal of sense to me. I had become more interested in such activities as playing basketball and trying to get my learner's permit. And better yet, I had come to fully appreciate the tantalizing possibilities that tickling Angela Fanelli held.

When I arrived at the Medicare stage of my life, I was certain that the fact that I didn't possess any musical skills was something that could not be remedied. I was of the opinion that I simply didn't have the energy or desire to learn to play a musical instrument. I wasn't so old that I had forgotten my strong distaste for practicing, but I did realize that practicing was still probably rather important if I was going to develop any kind of musical talent.

It was a painful realization. Even though I knew I didn't want to put in the hard work to learn to play the piano or saxophone well enough so I would be asked to entertain at a party, if I ever finally got invited to a party, I still felt badly when I thought about what could have been.

On the other hand, since I still did sing in the shower, it dawned on me that perhaps singing might be my last hope. Granted, it was a very long shot, primarily because my singing had not shown even the slightest bit of improvement over the years, but it still was a shot. If only I could find a way to improve my vocal performance in some quick, easy and cheap way.

I was quite certain that there was not anything out there that would meet my criteria until one day I was reading a magazine in my doctor's office. As I was thumbing through the magazine while waiting for my doctor to return from the golf course, suddenly it jumped right out at me. The headline of the advertisement sent chills down my spine: "YOU CAN SING GREAT—IN JUST 7 DAYS." I was stunned. I pinched myself to make sure I wasn't dreaming.

While I knew my singing in the shower wasn't the greatest, there still might be hope. My wife said my singing was bad, but she never said it was the worst she had ever heard. I still had the fantasy that if *American Idol* allowed people to audition in the shower, I might be good enough to make the first cut and go to Hollywood.

Even though my singing in the shower was indeed suspect, the potential to sing "great" while staying dry was quite tantalizing to me. And best of all, there was no mention of a teacher in the ad, hence, no Mrs. Meanlady. There also wasn't any mention of practice. I was ecstatic.

The ad went on to state: "If you are not a good singer or even if you feel you can not carry a tune, you can learn to be a great singer in the privacy of your home or car." This program was definitely designed with me in mind. I not only couldn't carry a tune, I didn't recognize one when I heard it, but with this method, it apparently didn't matter.

The ad stated that I would be able to achieve this marvelous singing ability by simply listening to and reading a CD and book set created by top vocal teachers and professional entertainers. I don't recall the cost, but money was no object if I would be able to finally achieve a life without regrets. I simply wanted to accomplish the things the ad said I would be able to accomplish, and there were a lot.

1. "Gain the confidence you need to sing in front of others." Actually, that wasn't a major concern for me. It was the audience that needed confidence that they would be able to endure my singing.

2. "Stretch your vocal range." I was really glad to read that claim. I had always thought being a monotone could only be corrected through surgery.

3. "Create unique vibrato." Shucks, I would settle for a common vibrato.
4. "Yodel creatively." Now this was icing on the cake. Learning to yodel by itself would be fantastic, but to "yodel creatively"....Jay Z, Mick Jagger, and Lady GaGa, eat your hearts out.
5. "Sing first-rate falsetto." That skill alone would be my ticket to the most exclusive parties and maybe even a gig as Frankie Valli in *Jersey Boys* on Broadway.
6. "Do tricks with voice." Golly, I could become a great singer and a magician. If I didn't make it on *American Idol*, I would be a cinch on *America's Got Talent*.

I realized it all sounded too good to be true, and as it turned out, it was. Remember I said I read this magazine in my doctor's office? Well, as I started to tear out the ad to take home, I discovered the magazine was fifteen years old! The product being sold no longer existed.

So, still to my regret, I cannot play the piano, I cannot play the saxophone, and I cannot sing. But maybe I'm not too old to learn to cook. If I can master some really delicious hors d'oeuvres, I might get a party invitation after all. I'm assuming, of course, that cooking doesn't take a lot of practice.

Don't Lose Your Pocket Knife

When my first wife, who is actually my current wife and the only wife I've ever had, but at the time, just a girlfriend, asked if I wanted to come home with her at Thanksgiving to meet her parents for the first time, I said, "No, why would I want to do that? You are my girlfriend. I'm dating you, not your parents. Your parents live way far away and that's a good thing. Maybe we can just call at Thanksgiving."

Since I wasn't sure my girlfriend/soon-to-be wife completely understood my sense of humor, I didn't say any of those things out loud. The fact of the matter is that I most definitely wanted to meet Lana's parents. I realized that being invited to her home at Thanksgiving was a good sign, a very good sign for the future of our relationship. But since I am an extremely shy person, I also realized it would be the most terrifying experience in my life, up to that point anyway.

We did make the trip to meet her parents, as well as the rest of her family, at Thanksgiving. Dinner was to be at the house of her older brother. The thought of having to make conversation at the dinner table had my stomach in knots, but I had developed a plan I hoped would help me get through it. The success of my plan centered on there being a large turkey on the table. There was.

The large turkey was necessary because it would provide me cover. I planned to hide behind the turkey whenever possible so I wouldn't be drawn into any conversations. And if anyone went for some turkey and made eye contact with me, I pretended I dropped something on the floor and I went down to get it. Unfortunately, one of the big effects of my shyness is that I often become so nervous I tend to behave rather stupidly. I become an alphabet that is missing all of the consonants and two vowels.

Regardless of the sheer foolishness of diving under the table, that move actually proved to be quite successful, as well as affording me quite an adventure. Once under the table, I found several small children gleefully enjoying the fact that they were out of sight and out of mind. I was the most gleeful of all.

I realized the children had reasons different from mine for being under the table; therefore it was remarkable how quickly we all bonded. They really didn't care if I was one of the big people. Adult or not, they seemed to appreciate the fact that I also preferred the nether world under the table to the world above where one had to sit up straight, eat vegetables and make eye contact.

None of us had to justify our presence under the table, which I particularly liked despite the cramped quarters. We all were just there and no questions were asked. We had an unspoken allegiance. So regardless of our reasons why we were in our present location, we all took advantage of our position and very quietly began to tie together the shoestrings of all the "grown-ups." I partook of the nefarious action because, well, because at the time, I was nervous and stupid.

On the plus side, I had indeed bonded with the children. Even though my companions under the table realized I was indeed a grown-up, they sensed I was a different kind of grown-up. Since my actions apparently showed my difference, I didn't feel the need to explain the concept of "being shy" to them. I was accepted unconditionally.

While I suspect my behavior seemed a bit odd to Lana's family, at least to the adults in the family, I still survived my Thanksgiving visit. I'm not sure what was said in private family conversations, but no one openly said anything to me that made me cringe. Actually, I think some of the family just thought I liked to play games with the kids.

While I breathed a great sigh of relief after that Thanksgiving meeting, my relationship was put to an even greater test the next time we all met. That time would be Christmas. I think the expression best describing my situation would be "going from the frying pan to the fire."

During my Thanksgiving visit I was just the mysterious boyfriend, but the situation took on a drastically different quality at Christmas. No one knew how serious my relationship with Lana was at Thanksgiving, and my being under the table most of the time didn't shed any light on the subject, but it became more obvious during my Christmas visit. At that time, Lana showed up wearing an engagement ring.

After the showing of the ring, I quickly realized that hiding under the table would no longer be a viable option. I knew I would have to actually interact with my future in-laws. I also knew that I would be more comfortable undergoing acupuncture, having tattoos put on my eyelids, and singing the national anthem naked at the Super Bowl. But I realized a man in love has to do what a man in love has to do. I reached deep into my backbone and tried to pull up as much resolve as I could muster.

When it became time to open our Christmas gifts, it became apparent that I hadn't pulled up enough resolve. At first, I had been really looking forward to the exchange of gifts. My eager anticipation for the gift exchange was not for selfish reasons of receiving presents. On the contrary, I hoped this time would provide me with another opportunity to just fade into the background.

An essential part of my plan was for everyone else to receive their gifts before me. As each family member received their gifts—this next point is crucial—an enormous pile of creased, rumpled, twisted, torn and tattered wrapping paper would begin to accumulate right in front of me. I would be able to hide. There wasn't a turkey available. While the only possible flaw in my plan would be if I received the first gift, I had a gut feeling that would not happen.

Let me offer a life lesson here. If anyone ever says you should do this or that because they have a *gut feeling* it is the right thing to do, tell them to take a Tums or something. The fact of the matter is that *gut feelings* that foretell the future don't exist. Such an idea is an urban myth. It's a country myth. It's a myth everywhere people with guts happen to live.

How do I know a *gut feeling* is of no use in foretelling the future? For starters, I felt in my gut that I would not receive the first gift to be handed out. Well, I did get the first gift and I wanted to immediately sink under a big pile of wrapping paper, but such a pile didn't exist as yet.

As I took the present, my only thought was to rip it apart and start the necessary pile of paper as quickly as possible. I feverously ripped the paper from the package. To be quite honest, I don't recall what the gift was, but as I looked up to thank the giver for the gift, I found many sets of eyes staring right at me. As I looked around the room, every set of those piercing eyes looked at me in a way I had never before seen.

While I didn't realize it at the time, I later learned the looks were not just looks, but each and every one of them amounted to "The Look," an expression that every member of Lana's family had mastered at an early age. I tend to believe The Look was an inherited trait. The Look is given when someone needs to be politely notified that whatever he or she just said or did was pretty much silly or just plain wrong. The fact of the matter is that The Look amounted to a strong, but nonetheless compassionate, reprimand.

When I first got The Look, which was a collective response and therefore far more effective than a single effort, I was certain I had done something drastically wrong. I just didn't know what my transgression happened to be. I looked to Lana for help, but she cast her eyes downward in an embarrassed way. She clearly didn't want to be a part of the group display of The Look, but I did notice she was turning her engagement ring round and round on her finger. I sensed I was in trouble and it didn't take long for me to understand my plight.

As the handing out of the gifts continued, the error of my ways became readily apparent. When the second gift was handed out, it all became obvious to me. The person who received the gift looked at it, shook it a bit, and slowly reached into his pocket and pulled out a pocketknife. He then opened it up by very carefully cutting the tape from the package. Actually, "very carefully" is incorrect; diamond cutters are very careful. This procedure was so precise, so methodical, and so painstaking that I just knew I was watching a vascular surgeon at work.

Because I had used a take-no-prisoners approach when I had opened my present, I was horrified to see that every single member of Lana's family used a pocketknife when their turns came. My wife-to-be had neglected to tell me she was from a family of vascular surgeons. And in each and every case, once the paper was removed from the packages, it was neatly folded and placed in an orderly pile.

There everyone sat with a neat stack of folded Christmas wrapping paper in front of him or her. For myself, I sat behind a crumpled and torn pile of paper. It was so torn and crumpled, it was hard to imagine what purpose it had ever served.

I'm not sure how long the entire process took, but from my frazzled perspective, it lasted for hours and hours. The good news is that I did survive. Lana's family proved to be very understanding and very forgiving. I was never criticized for my destructive actions. I was never lectured on the correct method for opening Christmas presents.

Lana's family does not lecture. They do use the aforementioned Look, which, while making a strong point, is relatively harmless. And after using The Look, they engage in rather practical and sensible behavior, which surfaced at our next Christmas together. It was at that time the gift of choice for me was a pocketknife. Maybe not a subtle message, but delicately effective. They all clearly realized that shy people often need to be handled with kid gloves. Now I just have to be careful not to lose my pocketknives.

Astrology...Or, Should You Get Out of Bed ?

I used to read my horoscope the first thing every morning, but I don't do that anymore. It wasn't that I ever particularly believed my horoscope. Actually, the truth of the matter is that I just wanted to see what the stars said my day would be like because it could come in handy. If the prediction was that I was going to have a bad day, then any mistakes I made during the day would just be the result of my astrological fate, not any personal shortcomings. I would then use that "astrological fate" ploy to cover a multitude of sins. You know, a kind of "the-stars-made-me-do-it" defense for anything I might do wrong during the day, and believe me, I do something wrong every day.

Unfortunately, neither my boss nor my wife, the people most affected by my blunders, were horoscope kind of people and I discovered that blaming my mistakes on the stars didn't carry much weight with either one of them. It was apparent that I had to stop relying on my horoscope and come up with a better explanation for my bad days. I'm still working on that.

Even though I no longer open the paper every day to the horoscope page, my interest in horoscopes still remains. I find the fact that so many people are still fascinated by the mystical power of reading the stars to be amazing. Practically every newspaper and magazine in the country carries an astrology column. There are horoscope apps for cell phones and computer home pages. There is little doubt that the practice of astrology is still popular despite the fact it is seldom accurate and rarely makes any sense.

Now I am not an astrologer and I've never played one on TV,

but I'm convinced I could write horoscopes that are just as good as the ones written by the professional astrologers. In fact, I think I'll do it right now. And if your boss and wife are believers, you might be able to use your horoscope to explain why you lost the big contract or forgot to take out the trash. It's worth a try.

ARIES (March 21 – April 19): Lady Luck could be smiling on you today. You will win the lottery or the Publisher's Clearinghouse Sweepstakes. But then again, Lady Luck actually may be smiling on the big doofus with *twenty-one* items who is standing in front of you in the "twelve-items-or-less" line at the grocery store. Kick this person in the shins so he will bend over and Lady Luck can see you. If this plan doesn't work, sue the store for violating its "twelve-items-or-less" policy. You may get some money after all.

TAURUS (April 20 – May 20): Your charm will rule your actions today, which will no doubt surprise everyone you know. Take advantage of your ability to attract members of the opposite sex. Comb your hair, skip the garlic bread at breakfast, lunch, and dinner, and stop challenging strangers to belching contests. Practice saying, "Hey, baby, what's your sign?" Seek out Aries people because they may be rich today.

GEMINI (May 21 – June 20): You are vulnerable today. Your ability to make intelligent, or even semi-intelligent decisions, will be lacking, but this shouldn't come as a surprise. Beware of Taurus people who come up to you and ask, "Hey, baby, what's your sign?" Beware of *anyone* who still says, "Hey, baby, what's your sign?" Libras will ignore you all day because that's just the way they are.

CANCER (June 21 – July 22): Emphasis on education, travel, and sports. You will be called to school when your vegetarian daughter starts a food fight in the cafeteria after finding a meatball in her salad. The football coach will be on lunch duty. After seeing your daughter thump the football player who put the meatball in her salad, the coach will ask her to join the team as a linebacker.

LEO (July 23 – Aug 22): Be positive. Be true to your word. Say what you mean. Keep your promises. Avoid deciding to run for president of the United States of America because the stress of being positive, being true to your word, saying what you mean, and keeping your promises will be way too much to bear. Pisces people will play a role and Cancer people will not because they all will be at school participating in a food fight.

VIRGO (Aug 23 – Sept 22): You will be facing a good news/bad news scenario. The good news is that you will get an unexpected sum of money. The bad news is that it will be your severance pay. An unexpected visitor will come to your house tonight. Make sure your theft insurance is paid up. Leo people will not play a role because, in all honesty, they don't like you.

LIBRA (Sept 23 – Oct 22): The diet you have faithfully followed for the last two months takes a turn for the worst when you realize you still qualify to be a participant on *The Biggest Loser*. Don't panic. Have a milkshake and some doughnuts while you think of a way to get through this. Avoid skinny people with attitudes.

SCORPIO (Oct 23 – Nov 21): Someone will hack into your computer and steal your identity. Don't worry because they will immediately give it back. You should take it personally that not even a hacker wants to be you. Tell a Libra person they look great and maybe they will like you.

SAGITTARIUS (Nov 22 – Dec 21): Lunar aspect coincides with fashion and style. Now is the time to start wearing clothes that match. Emphasis on personality and romance, but with your personality, you will have very little romance. Maybe the matching clothes might help. Study Taurus message even though it has absolutely nothing to do with you. Actually, it has very little to do with Taurus people either. They can be so gullible.

CAPRICORN (Dec 22 – Jan 19): Focus on budget matters. If you manage to balance your personal budget, call the President and Congress and tell them how you did it. If they don't understand what you did, take out a crayon and draw them a picture. That should help if you talk slowly and make big letters.

AQUARIUS (Jan 20 – Feb 18): This is no longer the Age of Aquarius. Get a life. You will exhibit sex appeal today. Go to work naked. Tonight features popularity and social activity. You'll be the center of attention, especially if you stay naked. Stay away from Aries, Taurus, Gemini, Virgo and Pisces people, as well as hungry lions. If staying away from hungry lions sounds like an idea you'd never thought of before, you probably are pretty stupid.

PISCES (Feb 19 – March 20): Focus on ability to enjoy work. Put a whoopee cushion on everyone's chair at the board of director's meeting and unscrew the top of the salt shaker when your company's most important client asks for the salt at lunch. People will think it is funny...the same people you will soon meet in the unemployment line.

IF TODAY IS YOUR BIRTHDAY: Success will follow you wherever you go, unless you decide to open your front door and go outside. Actually, to be safe, just stay home...in bed...under the covers...lock the door...disconnect the phone...Happy Birthday.

And the Winner Is...?

A wards shows on television annoy me for a variety of reasons, not the least of which is that so many people have an inexplicable fascination with the clothes being worn by the winners, losers, and those who were not-even-close-to-being-nominated. Because of this fascination with famous people and their attire, there are numerous TV programs that thrive on covering the red carpet part of the awards telecasts.

These shows bring in fashion experts to make sure the viewers know whether or not Angelina or Lady Gaga have made a fashion faux pas or deserve a "work it out girl." The latter apparently is very high praise. It seems that the people who stroll down the red carpet have absolutely no idea of how to recognize the difference between a pretty and an ugly dress. Fortunately, the fashion experts are there to explain the difference to the fashion-challenged, which apparently includes everyone except them.

I'm not really sure what makes one a fashion expert. Considering the way the fashion experts themselves are dressed, I'm pretty sure it involves being able to take vastly different articles of clothing, clothes that to the untrained eyes of the aforementioned fashion-challenged people would never be worn together, and then wear them together. Oddly enough, the fashion experts never seem to critique each other's clothes.

It seems that another requirement for being a fashion expert is the use of hyperbole. For example, when commenting on the attire of a celebrity, experts are given to such a phrase as "her dress was a disaster." Fashion experts apparently are unable to distinguish between the sinking of the Titanic and Meryl Streep wearing a gown that supposedly doesn't highlight her skin tone. I guess disasters are in the eyes of the beholder.

On the other end of the scale, the fashion experts are probably at their exaggerated best when they describe the clothes they like. Dresses are lauded as being "amazing" or "gorgeous." I even heard one dress described as being "elegant and easy." I know what "elegant" means, but I wasn't sure what made the dress "easy." I assumed it used Velcro strips as a fastener instead of a zipper. Surely that would be easy.

Fashion experts also feel compelled to comment on what the men who attend these award ceremonies are wearing. Such commentary is pretty much an exercise in futility because men's clothing is rather basic and the styles are not subject to much in the way of drastic changes from one year, or decade, to the next.

Actually, critiquing the women's apparel on these shows is also rather futile, at least to the males in the audience. While women may appreciate the differences from one gown to the next in terms of beading or lace detailing, to men it is all about the cleavage. Cleavage clearly trumps whether a dress is a Donna Karin or Donatella Versace.

In point of fact, all of the comments made about clothes as the stars slowly make their way down the red carpet, always trying to put their best side to the camera, is clearly not important to men. In reality, men prefer watching red carpet coverage with the sound turned off. Low-cut dresses speak for themselves.

Even though the overly opinionated fashion experts greatly annoy me, I think my biggest problem with awards programs is that they always give recognition and praise to the already rich and famous. They are a classic example of the rich getting richer, so to speak. There really needs to be an awards show for the little guy, the man on the street who does his job day in and day out for small pay and even less recognition.

For example, if I had my way, there would be the Mr. Goodwrench Awards Show for Auto Mechanics. It would be an annual awards ceremony right up there with the Oscars, the Tonys, the Emmys, and every other awards ceremony that exists for the greatly compensated and heavily pampered. I can envision the very first show, as the host revs the audience up for the grand finale.

Host: And now, ladies and gentlemen, it's time for the award we have been waiting for all night. With due respect to the oil changers and the tire rotators, it is now time for the Small Garage Auto Mechanic of the Year.

The first nominee is Big Boy Bernie Wilson for his sterling performance the time he repaired a 1960 Rambler that had carburetor problems. What makes his feat so amazing is that he did it despite a blaring radio in the garage, numerous distractions from waiting-room customers, an angry dispute between his watchdog and a cat sitting in the back of a car waiting to be inspected, and last, but not least, a tremendous hangover.

The second nominee is Bubba Joe Carson, who did a marvelous job when he fixed a flat tire on a 1995 Lincoln owned by a little old lady. He sold her a retread from a 1966 Volkswagon, convinced her the tire cost $500, and then managed to hide a large quantity of moonshine in her trunk for transportation across the state line.

The third and final nominee is Pedro Valdez. Pedro managed to fix a Honda that broke down in front of his garage in Cancun. The car was owned by a couple from Florida. Pedro's achievement was astounding considering he didn't speak English and the couple didn't speak Spanish. Despite the communication barrier, Pedro still discovered the cause of a 'pinka-pinka-plucka' sound that was coming from the engine, which he fixed using a paper clip, rubber band, and bottle cap from an orange soda.

Before I announce the winner, I'd like to comment on what our nominees are wearing tonight. Bubba Joe's plaid work shirt is by Wal-Mart and it is stunning, yet simple...

Now that would be an awards show worth watching.

Shop Until You Drop, But Don't Break the Law

When you greet the new day after a sleepless night caused by a Thanksgiving meal of too much turkey, dressing, and that stuff Aunt Freida made, the official start of the Christmas season has begun. The day is called Black Friday. You can choose to go shopping or eat leftovers, with each alternative being a losing proposition. You lose by shopping because of the overwhelming crowds and you lose by eating leftovers because of that stuff Aunt Freida made.

I'm not exactly sure how the first Friday after Thanksgiving became the official start to Christmas shopping, but I suspect the idea was the brainchild of folks like Mr. Penney, Mr. Sears, and Mr. Macy. Regardless of where the idea originated, the purpose of having an official beginning to Christmas shopping obviously was to create an atmosphere in which people would want to spend money, lots of money.

While storeowners didn't originate the idea of gift giving at Christmas—thank you, Magi—they have definitely fine-tuned it into an extensive and expensive tradition. Actually, it is rather amazing how a biblical reference to gift giving has been turned into a multi-billion dollar business. Are American entrepreneurs great, or what?

But despite the fact that the first day after Thanksgiving has long been accepted as the start of the Christmas-shopping season, some stores, no, many stores, no, a heck of a lot of stores, try to put people into a "don't-wait-until-the-last-minute-to-break-out-the-plastic" kind of mood long before that time. Surely their actions amount to entrapment. Enticing people to start Christmas shopping before Black Friday clearly goes against long-established tradition.

It is not uncommon at all for the push for early Christmas shopping now to begin before Halloween. I must confess that I find it rather annoying when stores sell Santa Claus masks for trick-or-treating! Any kids who show up at my doorstep dressed up as Santa or Rudolph do not get any candy from my "A" basket. They will get a pretzel stick and like it.

This action by the overeager stores does give rise to a few important questions. For example, are those stores that put up decorations and play Christmas music prior to the first official day of shopping acting in an illegal capacity? Are such businesses in violation of some sort of entrepreneurial law?

More importantly, what of the people who fall victim to this pressure to shop early? If they buy gifts before the official starting date, are they criminals? Are the purchased gifts to be considered stolen goods? I mean, good golly, imagine how embarrassing it would be to give Uncle Ferd a necktie purchased before Black Friday only to have the police interrupt the family celebration on Christmas morning to arrest the gift giver and confiscate the tie. Uncle Ferd might be glad to see the tie go away, but he surely would miss the person who gave him the illegally purchased cravat. Would the perpetrator of the crime be charged with a felony or a misdemeanor? Perhaps it depends on how ugly the tie was. What if it was a felony and the gift giver had to spend time in jail? Just imagine the shame of having to admit to the crime to a fellow prisoner.

"Hey, buddy, what are you in for? I slugged and robbed a Salvation Army bell-ringer."

"Well, uh, I bought a necktie for a Christmas gift before the official Christmas season had started."

"What! What kind of animal are you? At least I waited until after Thanksgiving before I slugged and robbed the bell ringer. Guard! Guard! Get me out of this cell with this piece of slime."

Pretty frightening, huh? Well, I know I'll never find myself in such a horrible situation. I am definitely not an early-Christmas-shopping kind of guy. But if such a law would ever be enforced, I would be worried about my sister-in-law. This lady has made early Christmas shopping a fine art. If arrested, charged, and put on trial, she definitely would be convicted. She starts her shopping so early that they would open Alcatraz again so she could serve her lengthy sentence there. But not to worry. If they don't have a gift shop, she would find her way out!

How to Beat Cabin Fever

I don't often get bored, but there have indeed been occasions when I was definitely at a loss as to how to pass the time of day. Bad weather is usually the culprit when I find myself in such situations. Too much snow or too much rain can make me a prisoner in my own home and it doesn't take too long before I feel that there doesn't seem to be anything to do. My usual "I've-got-some-free-time" pursuits such as watching TV or reading a book get old quickly. I find that I need something new and different to do.

I realize there are many really cool video games out there that can make time go by very quickly. I don't have any of those games. I don't have Xbox or Wii. Considering that I was never able to successfully play PONG, I would just be wasting my money if I attempted to become a member of the hi-tech game generation. My chances of being a *Guitar Hero* or defeating bad guys in *Modern Warfare* are about as good as my chances of being adopted by Angelina Jolie. I'm more likely to be adopted by Roseanne.

The bottom line is that I always need something else to help me deal with what is just old-fashioned "cabin fever." Consequently, over the years I have developed a variety of activities that help me pass the time of day when going outside the house is not an option. I want to share some of these activities because I'm pretty sure there are many people who will at some point find themselves trapped inside their home.

So, to help you maintain your sanity when you are falling victim to "cabin fever," I recommend trying some or all of the following:

1. Pierce your dog's ears and then insert rhinestone-covered doggie bones. If you don't have rhinestone-covered doggie bones available, since they really aren't very common, glue large grains of sea salt to regular doggie bones. I'm pretty sure Martha Stewart would approve this project.

2. Research the history of the toothpick. If you are going to be stuck in the house, you might as well turn it into a learning experience. Imagine how impressed people will be at a party when you take an hors d'oeuvre, eat it, and then as you look at the now-empty toothpick you begin to give a thirty-minute dissertation about the origins of the tiny piece of wood you are holding in your hand. Believe me, when word gets out about the things you know, you will find yourself on the guest list of a lot of parties.

It works for me. Okay, no it doesn't. The fact of the matter is that I don't get invited to parties because I still can't sing, play a musical instrument, and apparently I am not a charming conversationalist. The only party I ever attended came to a quick end after I stood in front of everyone and gave a lengthy discourse on the importance of using parsley as a garnish in order to make even unedible dishes at least look nice. On second thought, maybe you should just keep your wealth of knowledge about the toothpick to yourself.

3. Call every restaurant in the Yellow Pages and ask if they have fried jellyfish on the menu. If they do, make a note to never go there.

4. Begin writing an unauthorized biography of Lassie. I'm sure everyone knows that many different dogs played Lassie down through the years. But what probably isn't as well known is that the female character Lassie was always played by a male dog. What's up with that? Obviously there were not enough feminist dogs during the heyday of *Lassie* to protest a female being portrayed by a male. I really think there is an intriguing story here.

5. Arrange your canned goods in reverse alphabetical order. If this doesn't prove to be much of a challenge, set a time limit.

6. Write a musical comedy about the life of Calvin Coolidge. I'm sure most people think President Coolidge's life doesn't exactly lend itself to the Broadway stage, but I disagree. I can see the closing number right now, "Silent Cal Ain't Silent No More." With the right music and lyrics and choreography, it will bring down the house.

7. Write haunting ballads for the accordion or kazoo. Just the other day, in a conversation with some friends, we all concluded that there really isn't enough good music for the accordion or kazoo. Oh, I guess there is a plethora of hard rock stuff, but not enough tender, soothing ballads.

8. Perform cards tricks for your dog, after you teach him/her to pick a card. While this activity is difficult enough by itself, it could be extremely hard if your dog has not forgiven you for the pierced ears.

9. Try to remember your fifty favorite "knock-knock" jokes. If you can do this, then you should call a stranger and tell them all fifty jokes. If this person allows you to tell all fifty jokes, try to sell them some land you may or may not have in Florida.

10. Plan a vacation to Boise, Idaho, or any town named Boise in any state. If you have already been to a town named Boise, call a friend and tell them every detail of the trip.

11. Call CNN and ask "What's happening?" and then call The History Channel and ask "What happened?" Assuming they know their stuff, these calls could kill a lot of time. If The History Channel balks, tell them everything you know about the toothpick.

12. Write rap lyrics to Beethoven's Fifth Symphony. Call Kanye and Taylor Swift to see if they will do a duet of the number.

13. Write a letter to the Academy of Television Arts and Sciences and inquire as to why Bob Denver of *Gilligan's Island* never won an Emmy as best actor. Ask if they will

give Denver the award posthumously.

14. Talk to your houseplants about the consequences of unprotected sex. No one should have to face the hardship of unwanted jade plants.

15. Write a thank-you note to the IRS. Be sure to tell them how much you enjoy paying taxes. If it turns out you are getting money back, request an audit. I'm sure your letter will be passed around the office. Even IRS people need a good laugh now and then.

Okay, there you have it, a list of activities that are guaranteed to overcome even the worst case of "cabin fever." Heck, you may find yourself wishing for a rainy or snowy day so you can complete some of the activities that you started previously but didn't have time to finish.

The Lady at the Local Art Museum

It was called Sublime Effervescence.
There were lines and shapes and
dots and blurry things and many colors.
The lady at the desk said the painting
won a prize.
Blue Ribbon.
Best In Show.
The judges had all agreed.
She said it was magnificent and
didn't I agree?
She was certain it was the artist's best work and
didn't I agree?
When she finished swooning,
I asked what the painting meant to her.
She talked about the incredible use
of color and shapes,
pointing out that the artist had mastered
lines and dots and blurry things.
I nodded and looked closer.
She began swooning again and said
the painting cried out to her and
didn't it speak to me?
I said my hearing was bad,
so I wasn't sure.
The door opened and a new patron entered.
The lady ran to meet him.

I examined Sublime Effervescence once more
and wondered how anyone would know if the artist
had perfected blurry things.

The Way Things Ought to Be

When a new year approaches, newspapers and magazines are rife with columns and articles by psychics. While these seers do make predictions throughout the year, they seem to do most of their work just before the ball drops in Times Square. Evidently their psychic abilities are at their peak at this time, so they feel compelled to make predictions when they are at the top of their game, and newspapers and magazines feel compelled to print those predictions.

Now I'm not sure what qualifies a person to be a psychic. It seems that one just needs to make guesses about what might happen in the future. Apparently the "guesses" don't even have to be "educated." And they definitely don't need to be right. While a lot of attention is given to the predictions the psychics make, rarely are there ever any follow-up stories about whether or not the predictions come true. It turns out that accuracy isn't all that important. So the only thing a psychic needs to do is to make lots of predictions with the hope that perhaps two or three prove to be correct.

Since the magazines and newspapers that print the predictions have little interest in accuracy, they just focus on the most sensational looks into the future. The wilder and crazier the prediction, the better. Wild and crazy apparently sell more newspapers and magazines.

Because of this pressure to make sensational predictions, most psychics are prone to emphasizing gloom and doom when they look into a crystal ball. They make predictions that focus on disasters. They like to predict things like droughts, the end of the earth, and alien invasions. Surprisingly enough, alien invasion predictions always sell a lot of magazines and newspapers, especially if the aliens impregnate a famous actress or a powerful politician's wife.

I wish the editors of the newspapers and magazines who publish the absurd and ultimately inaccurate psychic predictions would have been my teachers throughout my years of struggle when I was in school. I would have found their indifference to correctness most welcomed since having the correct answers on tests or homework was not exactly my strong point.

For example, every one of the math courses I had in high school would have been so much better if my answers on homework and tests would not have been held to the rigid standards of accuracy that math people seem to cherish so much. Those rigid math folks didn't have the slightest bit of appreciation when I answered the question "What is pi?" with "a form of dessert best exemplified by delicious fillings atop a circle of crust."

At least my English teacher would have admired my use of the word "exemplified." Actually, my English teacher would have been astounded I could use the word "exemplified."

And where was the love from my math teacher when I answered the question "What is the square root of 438?" with "the correct answer plus zero." That response at least illustrated some mathematical knowledge concerning the concept of zero. Math teachers never seemed willing to give partial credit for anything.

Getting back to psychics, I must confess in all honesty that I had some moments when I considered getting into their game, but I was turned off by all of the negativity. I realized that I much preferred to concentrate on what I wanted to happen in the new year, something always positive, as opposed to fear mongering, which stressed the negative.

I'm simply not a gloom and doom kind of guy. I am a dreamer. I prefer the optimism achieved by trying to envision a better world. I want to think about the good things that I want to happen. And who would really want bad things to happen anyway? Well, maybe Chicago Cubs fans, and of course, psychics.

And if those things I would like to happen in the future were to actually occur, what a far better world it would be. Well, after careful consideration, I finally decided that I want to be a psychic, but a new kind of psychic. I want people to look at my predictions and have hope for the future. I want people to actually look forward to my predictions coming true. Accuracy will matter. So sticking with my positive outlook for the future, these are the things that I would like to see happen in the upcoming year:

1. A magazine that doesn't contain a single article about Brad and Angelina.
2. A session of Congress where everyone shows up and votes are actually taken.
3. Cheaper postage stamps. (I guess I've totally lost touch with reality on this one.)
4. A Republican say to a Democrat, or vice versa, "Hey, that's a great bill you have there. I think we need to pass it immediately."
5. A weatherman say, "Heck, your guess is as good as mine."
6. A pro athlete say, "I should get a pay cut because I didn't have a very good season last year."
7. A positive thirty-second political ad on TV.
8. A Pavarotti video on MTV.
9. The Energizer bunny come to a complete halt.
10. Mick Jagger sing the national anthem at the Super Bowl.
11. Toothpaste that just fights cavities.
12. A politician at a news conference answer a question by saying, "Wow, what a great question. I don't have the slightest clue as to the answer."
13. Cheerleaders for professional golfers. In fact, cheerleaders with megaphones doing cheers like "Make that putt. Make that putt."
14. Brussell sprouts becoming a banned substance along with heroin and crack.

I'm not saying that if my predictions for the future should actually occur we would have a perfect world, but it sure would be better than a world being invaded by flying zombie aardvarks ridden by evil trolls intent on destroying ice cream, fresh tomatoes from the garden, and the ability of teams in all sports at all levels to ever win a home game.

If You Ask Me

There doesn't seem to be a shortage of people who are more than willing to give advice on how other people should cut their grass, cook a turkey, or otherwise live their lives. This phenomenon has been going on since the time of cave men. Actually, the first cave man, who was named Grog.... "Wait a minute," you are probably yelling right now, "how do you know his name was Grog?"

Well, just relax. I wouldn't make such a statement without scientific evidence. "The-first-cave-man-was-named-Grog" assertion was in fact recently confirmed at the Anthropological International Symposium on First Names for Cave Men.

After an entire day of scientific presentations by some of the world's leading anthropologists concerning the name of the first cave man, the meeting was adjourned without a final resolution on the weighty matter. Everyone headed over to Big Louie's Bar for Scientists and Truck Drivers. After consuming numerous glasses of the happy hour special, aptly named The Big Bang Eighteen Wheeler Bomb, which primarily consists of diesel fuel and cheap beer, the by then thoroughly lubricated anthropologists unanimously voted on "Grog" as the name of the first cave man.

Percival Dumpkin had been selected to present the official scientific paper at the next morning's session of the symposium. He did. And it turned out he was the only anthropologist who showed up for the morning session. Percival voted in favor of accepting the paper and therefore Grog indeed became the name of the first cave man. It was scientific. Well, at least it was official.

Anyway, if I may regress, the most amazing part about people giving other people advice is that there are actually people who seek this advice and others who are paid to give it. The intriguing part of this scenario is the people who get paid.

Such people most often ply their remarkable trade in the print media. The people giving the advice receive letters from folks with some deeply troubling problems, all of which are so frightfully complex the quandary they find themselves in has left them totally unable to act. They are so at a loss as to what they should do, they are willing to wait weeks or months before they actually receive the advice regarding their horrible situation. That's how long it takes for the professional advice-giving folks to get around to answering their thousands of letters and having those answers printed.

What makes this "you-ask-for-advice-and-then-get-the-advice" practice so incredible is that the advice given to solve the problems is often inadequate. Now I will admit that some of the problems are truly perplexing, but I still find the advice given to deal with these distressing matters just as perplexing.

While I am not the wise man sitting on top of the mountain, I still feel I could give much better advice than most of the people who do the job now. For the most part, these people are determined to give advice that will not offend anyone. Considering the dweebs who write in asking for advice, there are indeed many times when being offensive is the way to go. I am willing to offend people when it is necessary, assuming they don't know where I live. To show you what I mean, check out how I would handle the following letters from pitiful people seeking solutions for their chaotic lives.

Dear Roger:

I just discovered that my wife is having an affair with my best friend. My oldest son is a drug dealer. My youngest son's room is full of pornography. My daughter wants to be a stripper. Last night the police came to the house to tell me my father had been arrested for making obscene phone calls to Nancy Pelosi. I'm at the end of my rope. What should I do?

Signed,

Worried in Washington

Dear Worried:

First of all, stop whining. Do you think you are the only person in the world who has problems? Don't you ever watch *Maury* or *Jerry Springer*? For heaven's sake, man, Maury had a woman on his show who named seventeen men as the possible father of her child. The father turned out to be her husband, who thankfully had at least made the list of seventeen. The other sixteen were guys who just happened to drive by the corner where the wife liked to stand every night.

Jerry had a man who loved his brother's wife but she loved her aunt's boyfriend, who actually was her third cousin twice removed on her father's side before he had a sex change and became her second mother. That may not make sense, but they all showed up on the show and fought each other. At least you haven't made a fool of yourself on TV. So quit complaining! The fact of the matter is that dysfunction is very much in nowadays. Maybe you should just get a reality show of your own and at least make some money.

Dear Roger:

Our neighbor and his pet gorilla like to play Frisbee in the backyard. Unfortunately, the gorilla doesn't catch very well, so when he misses, which he frequently does, the Frisbee comes into our yard. When the gorilla comes to retrieve it, he stomps through the flowers and sometimes he steps on the children. None of the kids have been seriously injured and the doctors say little Joey will be able to have children after all, but many of the azaleas have been destroyed. How can we politely tell our neighbor, who actually is a nice guy, to keep his gorilla in his own yard?
Signed,
Gone Ape in Philadelphia

Dear Gone Ape:

One would think that Philadelphia would have a leash law, but since that doesn't seem to be the case, you still have several options. I suggest you try the following:

1) Build a really, really strong fence.
2) Dig up the azaleas and plant a cactus. The cactus won't actually stop the gorilla, but you won't miss the cactus as much as the azaleas.
3) Buy a gorilla-hating elephant, a huge gorilla-hating elephant.
4) Teach the gorilla to catch.
5) Move to another neighborhood.
6) Go on *Jerry Springer* and fight the gorilla.

Not bad, huh? I think I give great advice. But since no one wants to pay me, I guess I'll just have to keep giving my sage wisdom to my neighbor. I'm going over there right now. I watched him wash his car the other day and he did it all wrong.

The Importance of Being an Expert
on the Antiques Road Show

I want to be an expert on old things,
not old things like great-grandparents
or even park bench people,
but the old things that are taken to the
Antiques Road Show
by
curious/optimistic/greedy folks
who
want their possessions to be valued
beyond being a family keepsake
that has been hoarded in a cluttered corner
of
the attic
or
secured in a box placed in a dark spot in
the basement.

My expertise may help them smile or laugh
or shout with joy, their desired reward for
continually saving stuff.

In my position as an expert on old things,
not old things like crazy Aunt Sally who
talks to squirrels, robins and wrens,
but the old things that are purchased at
yard sales

by
frantic, obsessed people
who
want to get a deal on some item that the
seller feels is nothing but a piece
of junk but actually might possess great value
to
informed eyes
or
even the sanguine eyes of
eager collectors.

My knowledge may ensure the belief that
one man's trash is another man's leap
into another tax bracket.

By being an expert on old things,
not old things like the McDonald's
early-morning breakfast crowd,
but the old things that are found at
antique shops
by
quiet, deliberate seekers
who
want to purchase a scarce object,
some truly rare find that will sell
at a price that will greatly increase
in
the future
and
even turn a nice profit in
the present.

My ability to see value in relics may
justify the cluttering of many houses
with things very hard to dust.

As an expert on old things,
not old things like mall walkers
who don't stop, shop, or even look,
but old things that are tangible examples of
long-held desires
of
expectant folks
who
yearn to achieve a sudden windfall that,
if handled correctly, will provide
a most welcomed financial security
for
the family
and
help them achieve the
American Dream.

My expertise may let them fulfill the
American Dream...but
only as these present-day patrons of happiness
now perceive it,
not as the tireless creators of these treasures
had lived it.

Who's Your Daddy?

Several of the afternoon reality TV shows are in a bit of a rut. No, actually, the Grand Canyon is a rut, the location of these programs is in a far, far deeper place. The exact location of that place is certainly open to debate.

Personally, I have a problem with these shows and that problem is that they have become obsessed with issues that can only be settled with DNA tests as those tests are used in paternity cases. I certainly appreciate the incredible advances that have been made in science, but I prefer that this particular scientific advancement would be used to determine something like the guilt or innocence of criminals.

Using DNA tests to discover which of several men might be the father of a child that resulted from consensual sex with a woman who apparently agreed to far too many sexual liaisons seems to be a misuse of science, as well as the airwaves. I find this "who's-your-daddy" emphasis in show after show to be most annoying.

To be quite honest, I am a bit astounded by this situation. I am not astounded that there is a lot of unprotected sex occurring, but I am astounded that there are so many women who are willing to go on television and admit they are a part of it all. The women who seem to be having such a difficult time determining the father of their children need to do one of three things. First of all, and the most obvious response, is that these women really might want to stop having unprotected sex.

Secondly, if they choose not to stop engaging in such behavior, they need to document the date they have sex and they need to write down the names of the men they have sex with, if for no other reason, the information could be used for future reference when they appear on TV.

And the third response is that if they continue to engage in unprotected sex with a large number of men, they really shouldn't go on TV to make public their intimate behavior. Isn't divulging humiliating personal information the purpose of Twitter and Facebook?

Perhaps the thing that amazes me the most about this "who's-your-daddy" phenomenon is that people watch such programs. In fact, a lot of people watch. While it is all beyond my comprehension, the ratings for these shows are apparently really good.

While the ratings are quite good for now, I predict the audience will eventually drop faster than the stock market during the Great Depression if every show continues to deal with accusatory women and defiant men making public their arguments about who is a slut and who is a lowlife slacker. Even smut gets old.

If I am indeed correct in my prediction that the fascination with current shows will begin to fade, then now is the time to begin preparing replacement programming. I'm certain that in the very near future the audiences will begin to yearn for more sophisticated fare. Well, maybe "sophisticated" is a bit strong; you don't go from dirt to diamonds overnight. But the point is that if the viewing audience is ready for something different, I can help. In fact, I will help. That's just the way I roll.

So, in the spirit of making the afternoon television viewing experience better for everyone, I would like to offer the following suggestions for new afternoon reality programming. My shows will deal with issues that concern every thinking American. I do believe that audiences growing tired of shows centering on men and women fighting over paternity issues will welcome programs that feature the following:

1. Topless waitresses who aspire to winning a Nobel Prize in any category.

2. Politicians who admit they aren't sure what to do. (In case they can't find any guests for this show, they can air a rerun of a classic afternoon reality show episode called "Who Is the Daddy of My Eleven Children or Is Billy Bob the Daddy of Them All?")

3. Professional athletes who think they are overpaid. (In case this show can't find any guests, the back-up show would be a repeat of the classic "Women Who Really Believed Their Lovers Were Going to Divorce Their Wives.")

4. Teenagers who think their parents know more than they do.

5. Tall women who only date jockeys.

6. Teenagers who secretly listen to Yo-Yo Ma.

7. Twins who can't tell each other apart unless they dress differently.

8. Supreme Court justices who look at past decisions and say, "What was I thinking?" (Since Supreme Court justices like to avoid any form of public accountability, the back-up show would be a repeat of the classic "You May Not Be My Daddy, But Momma Likes the Car You Drive.")

9. Paparazzi who only take posed pictures of celebrities.

10. Doctors who think their patients pay way too much money. (If there aren't any guests for this show, and there won't be, there will be a rerun of the classic "If You Really Loved Me, Why Did You Take My Dog, My Truck, and My Last Beer?")

11. Lawyers who think their clients pay way too much money. (The chances of this show ever making the air is close to impossible. In this time slot, there will be a repeat of the classic show "I Drive a Mercedes, How Would I Know I Was Supposed to Put Money in the Parking Meter?")

12. Politicians who think they are overpaid. (This show actually might have a guest or two. There is always some politician up for re-election who goes after votes by promising, if elected, to take a pay cut. When elected, that promise goes by the wayside with all of the other promises that were made.)

13. CEOs who think their bonuses should only consist of Taco
    Bell coupons and a pat on the back.

There you have it. I truly think my plan will rescue afternoon
television and there won't be any need for DNA testing, and better
yet, the fighting will probably be kept to a minimum. I suppose
there could be a bit of a tussle if the topless waitresses have a
disagreement on who should get the Nobel Prize in physics.

Section Two – My Favorite Operas

Like Section One, the name of this section is quite misleading. In point of fact, I don't have any favorite operas. The reason, quite simply, is because I dislike all operas. I'm pretty much an old school rock and roll guy, but I do realize that lovers of rock and roll and lovers of opera do have something in common. They both profess love for a form of music in which understanding the lyrics is quite difficult.

So, since I don't appreciate opera, why would I name Section Two "My Favorite Operas"? The answer is, I chose that name out of respect for my sister-in-law. She truly loves opera and I love her. We just don't go to concerts together.

The essays in this section are really about sports, a topic about which my sister-in-law knows very little. By "very little" I mean she knows absolutely nothing. I don't know much either, but I still do love just about all types of athletic endeavors anyway.

But now that I think about it, there actually is a connection between opera and sports. I wish I had a dollar for every time I heard some coach or sportscaster say about a game in which one team was trailing by a large score, "It ain't over until the fat lady sings!" That clearly is an opera reference by a sports person. But then again, maybe it is just a reference to Mamma Cass of the Mammas and Papas.

Three Strikes and You're Out

It isn't a "stop the presses" kind of news flash, but I'd like to report that baseball is no longer the national pastime. In fact, it hasn't been thought of in such a favorable light since I convinced my friend Froggy to give me his Mickey Mantle rookie card by telling him the Mick was quitting baseball to become a truck driver. That was over fifty years ago. Froggy was gullible then and he still is today. He now spends most of his time buying products advertised on TV that feature the phrase, "Wait! There's more!"

Baseball's fall from grace has been rather dramatic. Today the former number one ranks just below doubles Hula-hooping and just above professional pogo stick jumping. And it is entirely possible it will soon be surpassed by the fast-rising blindfolded Chinese checkers.

There are many sports pundits who point to the use of steroids by some of baseball's most successful players as the explanation for the game's decline. That assertion is too little, too late. Baseball's fall from grace began long before small players decided to become big players. And the reasons for the decline go far beyond players bending over to get clandestine injections of some body-enhancing drug instead of just drinking beer like the Great Bambino did.

The real reason for people turning away from baseball is much simpler. The game is slow. Perhaps I should be more specific. The game is incredibly slow.

Baseball simply cannot keep up with the fast pace of life today. In a world where people are enthralled with high-speed computers, multi-functional cell phones, and really good corkscrews, baseball has become an anachronism. People want things to happen now and the game of baseball falls short in satisfying that need.

Instead of highlighting the action that people come to the ballpark to see, such as hitting and running and throwing and catching, baseball players would rather fidget, spit, scratch, and spit some more. Being able to spit, particularly when on camera, seems to be what baseball players do best and most often, not counting the continual readjustment of the nondrinking cup each player wears in his pants.

The entire scenario is enough to even make a mime shout "Just play ball!" At least in auto racing when someone says "Start your engines," the competitors start their engines. In baseball, when they say "Play ball," the players first decide to fill their mouths with a bag of sunflower seeds.

Actually, eating sunflower seeds, as practiced by baseball players, is a remarkable skill. Once the seeds are put in the mouth, hands are no longer used, just teeth and the tongue complete the job. Cracking open a shell in a mouth full of shells, extracting the seed from the open shell, chewing the seed, swallowing, spitting out the now-empty shell, and starting the process all over again is an extraordinary feat. Unfortunately, this eating skill, as impressive as it is, clearly adds to the slowness of the game.

To completely understand the annoyingly slow pace of baseball, one just needs to look at how the most drama-filled moments in the game, those being the confrontations between the pitcher and batter, unfold. These head-to-head confrontations, which are at the heart of the game, are slow.

No, that's not exactly correct. Turtles making a cross-country trip from Virginia to California are slow. A seedling redwood tree growing to maturity is slow. An inchworm crawling up the Empire State Building is slow. But compared to pitcher-batter duels, all three are actually record-breaking sprints.

One would think that the batter would step into the batter's box and the pitcher would proceed to throw him pitches. But when it comes to baseball, thinking is not necessarily a strong point. Why else would one league use the designated hitter and the other not? Better yet, what happened to the thinking process when it was decided whichever league won the All-Star game would have home field advantage in the World Series?

Anyway, a typical pitcher-batter encounter begins slowly when the batter holds up the process by adjusting his batting gloves before he even steps into the batter's box. *Batting gloves?* Surely guys like Cobb and DiMaggio turn over in their graves every time a batter puts on the gloves and the Velcro is pushed tight. It's bad enough that today's player feels it is necessary to wear such gloves, but by doing so, the game is further slowed. Evidently it is extremely difficult to fit those gloves because batters continue to fiddle with them after every pitch, once the first pitch is actually delivered.

While continuing to fool around with his batting gloves, the batter intently stares down at the third base coach so he can see if he is supposed to swing or take the pitch when he finally decides to actually get into the batter's box. The message giving him the necessary information is delivered in a series of hand signals that involve the third base coach touching various parts of his body in some sort of meaningful sequence that conveys what he wants the batter to do.

Problems can arise if the coach should sneeze or swat away a fly or smack a mosquito on his hand. The batter immediately calls time, adjusts his gloves for the umpteenth time, and using another form of baseball's many secret languages, signals the coach the question, "What the hell was that?" The signal is performed by the batter extending both arms sideways, putting his palms up, hunching his shoulders, and putting a quizzical look on his face. The batter may also touch various body parts before, during, and after this signal in order to confuse the opposing team from deciphering what his message actually may be. And he will definitely spit throughout the entire process.

While the batter and the third base coach have been delaying the game by giving signals and misunderstanding those signals, the pitcher has tried to remain nonchalant. To show his lack of concern about the delay, he has been digging in the dirt on the mound, playing with the rosin bag, and using his cell phone to take a picture of some hot chick sitting in the front row.

Once the batter finally takes his place in the batter's box, the pitcher and catcher then begin their form of secret communications. Their secret language consists of the catcher showing a certain number of fingers in some sort of pattern that lets the pitcher know if he should throw a fast ball, curve, slider, or some other type of pitch in his arsenal. If the catcher should happen to hitch up his underwear during this process, the confused pitcher quite possibly will balk.

After receiving the catcher's signals, a pitcher sometimes replies with a gesture in which he quickly jerks his head from side to side. This headshake apparently means, "Hey, dude, what are you thinking? I don't want to throw that pitch." If he wants to disguise this message from the other team, the pitcher may spit.

The pitcher's rebuff of the catcher's suggested pitch usually leads to what is often a time-consuming meeting on the mound. It seems that pitchers like to decide what pitch to throw and catchers evidently are sensitive types who have major issues when their suggested pitch is rejected. The meetings on the mound are like mini therapy sessions where the two men try to deal with their issues. Or the meeting could really just be an opportunity for the pitcher to show the catcher the picture he just took of the hot chick in the front row. Both players end the meeting by spitting.

Sooner or later, most often later, the dramatic battle between pitcher and batter continues with actual pitches and swings being made. Regardless of the outcome of the confrontation, the pitcher gets a strikeout or the batter gets a hit or a walk, the two players will probably not get to face each other again in the ball game they are currently playing. The reason for the one time meeting in the game lies with the way pitchers are now used in baseball and it exemplifies yet another reason for the slowness of a baseball game.

In baseball, as it is played today, no one is simply a pitcher. That position has become much more specialized. Pitchers now are either starters, long relievers, short relievers, set-up men, closers, or guys who take the mound because there isn't anyone left in the bullpen. In this climate, before the start of the game managers are prone to say things like, "I hope to get five innings out of Smedley today."

Excuse me, five innings? Smedley makes $10 million a year, so if he's on my team, he better be ready to pitch both ends of a double-header and throw batting practice for the local Little League team. But since I don't run a team, I have to endure those who do run them by using their "let's-make-as-many-pitching-changes-as-possible" approach to baseball.

Once a starting pitcher makes his first pitch, he's fair game to be removed by the manager for just about any reason. Generally the decision to bring in a different pitcher is based on the next batter. For example, managers are hesitant to let a right-handed pitcher face a left-handed batter and vice versa. Go figure. You'd think a major leaguer making millions of dollars should be able to pitch to left- and right-handed batters.

Reasons for making a pitching change can even go far beyond which side of the plate a batter happens to stand. Some pitchers are not allowed to pitch to certain hitters if the temperature is above 70 degrees and the wind is five miles a hour out of the west, unless it is a Tuesday and the batter in question is under 6'2" and 220 pounds.

These decisions about what pitcher will face what hitter, and many others equally confusing to me, are made by overactive managers who in so many ways are the very cause of the lethargy that plagues the game of baseball today. The problem is that managers take their responsibilities way too seriously. Like coaches in all sports, baseball managers do not do anything athletically to affect the outcome of the game, but it seems to bother them more than it bothers coaches in other sports.

Since managers are distressed by their inability to run or hit or pitch or catch or in any physical way influence the game, they are obsessed with trying to show how smart they are. They use their superior thinking skills, as they perceive them to be, to tell batters when to swing, take a pitch, or bunt, outfielders and infielders where to position themselves, and runners when to steal. They change pitchers on a whim. They always argue with umpires even though they know the call will not be changed. They also send out the pitching coach to get the pitcher's cell phone so the manager can see the picture of the hot chick in the front row.

The one thing that managers do not control concerning the way players play the game is spitting. Players have the green light to spit whenever they want. That happens to be pretty much a player's God-given right that not even an egotistical manager would try to change.

The bottom line is that baseball managers try to insert themselves into the game more than any other coach in any other sport. Their insistence in attempting to control most aspects of the game only succeeds in slowing down the game, and in some cases, stopping it completely. Actually, it is not always easy to know if a baseball game is still going on or has been stopped. I have a friend who once sat through a two-hour rain delay and never knew it.

Now baseball fans throughout the country, especially the baseball "purists," become indignant when their favorite sport is criticized. They really need to relax and accept the fact that baseball is in the lower echelon of sports in America. While the game is not going to disappear from the face of the earth, the chances of it ever returning to its exalted place of relevance among American sports are very slim.

Thinly clad cheerleaders along the first and third base lines and nickel beer in the stands might help, but not enough. Short of drastic changes in how the game is now played, baseball simply cannot return to its glory days. The problem is quite simple. Baseball is now a five-page, handwritten letter trying to compete in a text-messaging world. It can't be done.

For a Kid, the Score Shouldn't Say It All

I didn't attend the game, but my friend, Pops, was there to watch a kid from his neighborhood play. It was a little league basketball game, but it could have been any sport. The game was played in Everywhere, USA.

For the purpose of distinguishing between the two teams involved, I will call them the Good Guys, obviously the home team, and the Bad Guys. Players on both teams were eight- and nine-year-olds, although on occasion a given player's age might come into question. The age disputes only arose if a player scored a sufficient number of points to actually impact the game's outcome. No points, and the kid could be old enough to drive himself to the game without anyone batting an eye.

At the particular game Pops described to me, everything began to happen with just ten seconds left on the clock. The Good Guys trailed by one point. They had the ball and their coach had just called a timeout.

Coach: Percy! Hey, where is Percy? I've got to get him in the game because of that stupid rule that says every kid has to play. Where in the hell is Percy?

1st player: Coach, my mom says you shouldn't curse.

Coach: Yeah, well your mother isn't under the pressure I'm under, kid. And furthermore, I'm a man and I'm a coach. Men coaches curse. It's part of the job description and it's genetic. So, begging your mother's pardon, where in the hell is Percy?

2nd player: He went to the bathroom.

Coach: The bathroom! Doesn't he know basketball players

aren't supposed to use the bathroom in crucial situations? Would Dirk or Kobe use the bathroom in the last ten seconds of a game?

2nd player: Well, if they...

Coach: No, they definitely would not! Now, where is Percy? If I don't get him in the game, we'll forfeit. That reminds me—you, fat kid, have you played yet?

3rd player: Yes, coach, don't you remember that you put me in the game during the last three seconds of the first quarter? It was right after you got the technical foul for giving the ref an obscene finger gesture and then saying something about his mother.

Coach: Oh, yeah, I remember now. That was really a lousy call he made. Just because Farnsworth went from the middle of the court to the free throw line without dribbling, he's going to call traveling. That clown has been calling them way too close this entire game. Anyway, right now, I need Percy. You, tubby, waddle down to the bathroom and tell Percy to get up here right now.

4th player: Hey, coach, here comes Percy.

Coach: Percy, hustle up here and go get in the game. But remember one thing, when you get out there, stay out of everyone's way. And whatever you do, don't touch the ball. We can win this game if you don't mess it up.

When play resumed, Pops said the scene was total bedlam. The Good Guys tried to inbound the ball against a torrid full court press. The kid taking the ball out of bounds couldn't find an open man except Percy. Forgetting the coach's instructions, the kid panicked and passed the ball to a very surprised Percy. This action caused the already overwrought coach to become even more agitated, something most people thought impossible.

Time started ticking off the clock as the coach and Percy's teammates started yelling at him to pass the ball. Ten. Nine. Eight. Instead, Percy whirled around and eyed the basket. And then, with a fierce determination in his eyes, he started dribbling straight for the goal. Seven. Six. Five.

One of Percy's teammates tried to steal the ball from him, but Percy put a great move on him and continued toward the basket.

Four. Three. Two. With everyone in the gym on their feet, Percy lofted a two-handed, underhanded shot. The form was definitely unorthodox, but the ball still went flying straight toward the basket.

Even though the horn sounded ending the game, the ball had left Percy's hands before the final blast, so his shot would count if it went through the hoop. The ball seemed to be moving in slow motion...super slow motion.

With everyone screaming at the top of their lungs, the ball finally reached its destination. It hit the rim and bounced straight up into the air. Slowly it began its descent, heading for the basket where it barely touched the rim again and fell harmlessly to the floor. The Good Guys had lost.

The coach stormed out onto the floor and demanded to know why Percy had shot the ball instead of passing. The rest of the team circled Percy, yelling that he had lost the game. Several parents told Percy he should quit the team because he was taking time from the better players.

The gym then quickly emptied and Percy was standing there alone when Pops walked up to him. "What a doggone barnburner that game was! Percy, you played a good game."

"What? A good game? We lost and it was my fault. I missed the last shot."

"Percy, the team lost, but it wasn't your fault. A lot of your teammates missed shots today, any one of them could have won the game."

"Yeah, well everyone yelled at me."

"I guess that's true, but that's because people just don't understand that the first missed shot is as important as the last missed shot. The main thing is that you are getting better."

"What do you mean? I still haven't scored. I always miss."

"First of all, that was some great dribbling you did getting the ball down the court against the press. And about that shot, well, it hit the rim."

"So? I still missed it."

"Percy, you missed, but you hit the rim. Don't you get it? Boy, you hit the rim and you've never done that before. You hit the rim; in fact, you hit it twice on one shot. You definitely are getting better and I know you will score some day. It might be next week or the week after, but you will score."

For the first time during this discussion, Percy's eyes lit up and he had a slight smile on his face. "You really think I might score some day? Really?"

"Percy, you will score. Now let's go get some ice cream and then I'll give you a ride home. How does that sound?"

"Great, that sounds great! I can't wait to tell Mom I hit the rim."

Pops put his arm around the now-smiling boy and they walked out of the gym together. The promise of youth had been restored for a small boy who was beginning to realize that the score shouldn't say it all.

The Agony of Defeat

Have you ever noticed how sports reporters are so aggressive in their interviews, particularly with a losing coach? While the victor in a particular competition gets first crack to express the jubilation of his victory, inevitably the loser also has to face the glare of the cameras. No doubt the losing coach would rather be alone somewhere crying in his beer, or at least drinking it. Instead, he finds himself being confronted by some sportscaster with a microphone.

It is as if these sports reporters, who constantly have to travel around the country, are trying real hard to find a permanent home sitting at an ESPN anchor desk. As a result, they are attempting to make an impression with the powers-that-be by showing how much they know about the sports they are covering. Often that knowledge is rather limited, considering they couldn't work up a sweat in a steam room let alone work up a sweat on an athletic playing field, something most of them never did.

The questions they ask more often than not amount to second guessing and are not an attempt to gain any real insight into the losing coach's emotions about the loss he just suffered. (Perhaps showing the coach crying in his beer would suffice.) Rather than displaying a hint of sensitivity and compassion to a coach who just minutes earlier felt the pain of having years of hard work go down the drain, the reporters focus on how victory could have been possible if only the coach knew as much about coaching as they did.

The entire process got me to wondering how the aggressive-know-it-all approach so often used by sports reporters would have played in other types of contests, say some of the great non-athletic confrontations of the past. Such thoughts stagger the imagination.

"Well, Goliath, it looks as if you really underestimated the little guy. Looking back now, don't you wish you would have trained harder? Let's face it, you were sluggish, flat-footed, totally out-of-shape. Is losing the championship worth all of the partying you did before the fight?"

"Emperor Napoleon! Hey, Emperor, do you have a minute? I'd like to ask you a few questions about the Battle of Waterloo. Hey, what's with the hand in the shirt? Do you have indigestion or something? No matter, that pose will make a great painting and posing is all you're going to be doing for quite a while. Anyway, what was the problem today? Wellington pretty much kicked your butt. Don't you think you should have stayed retired on Elba? Why is it so hard for you to see you don't have it anymore? Oh well, you can think about it on St. Helena."

"Gen. Cornwallis, the word is out that you plan to surrender tomorrow to Gen. Washington. As you well know, coming into the American Revolution, your troops were the overwhelming favorites. No one doubts your ability to command troops. Your men are always well disciplined and they execute flawlessly, but many people think your game plan was not well thought out. To cut to the chase, General, how will you answer the critics who say you can't win the big one?"

"Well, Pharaoh, it looks as if Moses really outsmarted you this time. Don't you think that if you would have simply let his people go, you wouldn't be so embarrassed and humiliated today? You were just out-coached. Why weren't you prepared for the parting of the Red Sea? Surely the staff into a snake move should have been a tipoff that Moses likes trick plays."

"Gen. Custer, can I have a moment before the second half begins? Considering how badly beaten your troops were in the first half, don't you think you need to make some major adjustments? Letting the Indians surround your men just doesn't seem to be working. What were you thinking with that strategy?"

Maybe people who have just experienced the agony of defeat

should just be left alone. Interviews with these people are, well, they are agonizing.

I Love Golf, But Golf Doesn't Love Me

Whoosh! Forget the buds that are beginning to appear on trees or the sight of brave little flowers breaking through the now-melting snow.

Whish! If you truly want to know that spring is about to arrive, just close your eyes and listen.

Thunk! The sound you will be hearing, the sound that clearly announces the arrival of spring, is the sound of me hitting golf balls in my backyard.

Whiff! Or, it could be the sound of me swinging at but missing golf balls in my backyard.

You see, I love golf. Unfortunately, golf doesn't love me. In fact, golf doesn't even like me. Heck, golf doesn't even acknowledge that I exist. Nonetheless, when the temperature begins to rise and the snow begins to melt, I still haul out my clubs and start preparing for yet another season on the links.

Even though I have been playing golf for many, many years, it seems that my only real accomplishment is an increased knowledge of the rules. I am an expert on the rules for losing a ball, having an unplayable lie, hitting into a lateral water hazard, and tossing a club that knocks a fellow golfer unconscious.

Concerning all of these rules, been there, done that, and will probably do it again. No, will definitely do it again. The point is that I know what to do in all of the aforementioned situations and many others that I didn't mention. In fact, I have even been involved in some situations that aren't covered by the rules because no one ever managed to do what I did.

In spite of my familiarity with the current rules, and the rules that will no doubt have to be created someday because of the havoc I am able to create on a golf course, the actual ability to play the game still eludes me. It appears that I have taken a difficult game and made it impossible.

This extremely distressing situation doesn't exist because of a lack of effort on my part. On the contrary, I continue to practice, practice, and practice. And yet, I still cannot properly execute a chip shot, hit a straight drive, blast out of a sand trap, or sink a two-foot putt. I even have trouble placing the ball on the tee. Many times I get lost on the way to the course.

Most golfers measure their success by whether or not they shoot a low score. I consider it a good day on the links if I don't lose a dozen golf balls…or lose a golf club…or forget where I parked the golf cart on any particular hole.

Some golfers can routinely reach long par-5's in just two shots. I'm excited when I get to a par-5, long or short, before sundown! But the fact of the matter is that I do indeed have a spectacular short game. Regardless of what club I use, I can hit it shorter than anyone I know. What can I say…it's a gift!

One would think that my lack of golfing skills would make me a golfing pariah. On the contrary, I am very much in demand on golf courses everywhere…throughout the nation…throughout the world. When I arrive at a course, there are usually long lines of men, women, and children waiting to play a round or two with me.

Actually, that's not exactly correct. They don't want to play *with* me; they want to play *against* me. Trust me, there is a big, big difference. The difference being that the great demand for me as an opponent instead of being a partner means I am an *easy mark*. In order to understand the concept of *easy mark*, one must first understand the phrase *taking candy from a baby*! These concepts come quite easy to people from Vegas or Atlantic City.

I suspect many of the people who can't wait to get a match against me actually use the matches as a second source of income. In fact, I am certain there are two little old ladies who use the money from their matches with me as their *primary* source of income. Their golf winnings from matches against me evidently are greater than their Social Security checks. I suppose I will have to start sending out W-2 forms to these ladies.

In the meantime, I'll continue to work on my golf game in my backyard. I really would like to reach a level where I don't have to yell "Fore!" every time I hit a shot...even a putt...especially a putt!

So even though my game is shaky at best and downright dangerous at worst, I'm not prepared to give up just yet. Furthermore, I have a big match this weekend with a guy who is in the process of buying a house. I think he is counting on me for the down payment! Well, he just might be in for a big surprise!

I believe I will get better and I believe someday Lucy will not move that football when Charlie Brown tries to kick it. It's all about attitude and I have a good attitude. And as I said, I do practice a lot. So, if you would please excuse me, I'm going out to do just that.

Kaplunk!

They Might Be Contenders

If your children want to go outside and shoot baskets or hit golf balls instead of doing their homework, let them. In fact, encourage them. Hide their textbooks and push your kids out the door and tell them not to come back inside until it is dark. Make it a rule that they play some game involving a ball rather than do math problems. If they break that rule, punish them, but only in a way that doesn't affect their putting stroke or ability to throw a football sixty yards or shoot a deep three-pointer with a hand in their face.

Some might think such advice is poor parenting. At best, it might seem to be some obscure form of reverse psychology to get children to do homework, or at worst, just plain stupidity. Actually, this counsel is a wake-up call for old school, do-your-homework parents who still cling to the outdated notion that an education is the best way to succeed.

The point is that my advice actually reflects the present state of professional sports today and that state is one of money and youth. It is crucial for parents to understand this fact because their understanding could lead to early retirement.

It is all really quite simple. Professional athletes are presently earning salaries greater than the gross national product of many countries, and most importantly, many who are being paid such large sums of money are very, very young. So young, in fact, that kids who only just recently were able to stay home without a babysitter are now signing multimillion dollar contracts to play games and wear a particular brand of athletic shoes. Some of the kids reaping these windfalls are so young they are signing their contracts with a crayon.

Besides the young age of these athletes, what makes this situation even more remarkable is that the level of play doesn't have to be particularly outstanding to command such huge salaries. Third-string quarterbacks make more money than their coaches. Baseball players who can't hit their weight still earn over a million dollars a year. Basketball players who ride the bench while wearing baggy shorts and more tattoos than the entire hip-hop generation and every member of the Seventh Fleet combined earn salaries that rival CEOs of top corporations. And they all make more money than educators, scientists, and the president of the United States.

It is obvious that despite the protestations of many team owners, there is a lot of money to be had in the world of professional athletics. Not only is there a lot of money available, there are many more opportunities to receive this money because of the expansion of franchises over the years. And since this expansion has led to a dwindling talent pool, it is easier to become a pro nowadays. Athletes who wouldn't have made the roster for the Podunk Porcupines in years gone by now play for big time teams and take home sums of money that would even get Bill Gates's attention.

The bottom line is that in the present climate, it appears that kids who prefer recess and gym to math and science may be showing a greater wisdom than their parents and teachers. It is apparent that playing "kids" games is now definitely a valid career choice, even if the player isn't the most athletic kid on the block.

The following conversation, which should be read by all parents, illustrates an extremely salient point concerning your child's future:

High school coach: Come on in, Joey. Have a seat. I called you to my office because there is a basketball scout from the NBA here to see you.

Joey: Someone from the NBA wants to see me?

High school coach: Well, not exactly. Actually he wanted to see Jumping Jerome Jackson, Sammy the Skyscraper, and Dunking Danny, but since they've already signed pro contracts, he said he'd talk to you.

Joey: Golly, coach, you'd think he'd want to see Willie the Water

Boy before he'd see me. Willie got into more games than I did.

Coach: As a matter of fact, he did want to see him, but Willie also has signed a pro contract. He got a deal to play for the new franchise in Secaucus, New Jersey. (Knock on the door.) There's Sam now. Come on in, Sam. Joey, this is Sam Skywalker. I'll leave you two alone.

Sam: Nice to meet you, Joey. Your coach has told me a lot about you. I think you just might be a good fit for our team, but there are a few questions I'd like to ask you. First of all, what was your scoring average this season?

Joey: Well, I only got to play in one game, but I did make a basket. My shot was a little low, but it bounced off my teammate Fat Freddy's head and it went right in. Freddy thought he should get credit, but heck, I shot the ball, low or not.

Sam: How many times did you shoot in that game?

Joey: Just once. No one would pass me the ball.

Sam: Hey, kid, that's a 100% shooting average. Impressive. Did you do anything else in the game? Get any rebounds?

Joey: I almost got one. I was in good position, but Fat Freddy got in my way and ended up pushing me into the bleachers just as the ball came off the rim.

Sam: That's too bad, but it's good to know you were in the right position for the rebound. Are you a good passer? Did you get any assists in the game?

Joey: Hey, if they won't pass the ball to me, then I'm not passing to them! I just like to do my own thing, if you know what I mean.

Sam: I know exactly what you mean. You're a take-charge kind of guy. You want the ball in your hands when the game is on the line. We need players like that. Okay, let's talk defense. Are you a good defensive player?

Joey: I don't know for sure. I only tried it once, but I got tired chasing my man all over the floor. I guess I might have some potential though. It's not like I totally passed out or anything.

Sam: Of course not, and you said the magic word, "potential." We in the NBA love potential. That's why we have a draft. Now, just one more quick question. What do you feel are the strong points of your game?

Joey: Golly, I haven't really thought about that. I never actually realized I had a game. Well, let me see, I'm real good at lining up on the free throw line. I've never jumped in the lane too soon. And what else, oh yeah, I can tie my sneakers so they stay tied.

Sam: Wow, lining up on the free throw line correctly is becoming a lost art. You'd be surprised at how many guys haven't mastered that kind of fundamental. And being good at tying your shoestrings is also great. Shoe manufacturers will love that. Okay, I think I've heard enough. Let's talk contract. Even though your statistics don't put you in the *great* category, like say, Jumping Jerome, or even in the *good* category—the water boy had those kind of stats—I think you just might have the potential—remember that magic word—to possibly become a journeyman type of player. We are willing to take that chance on you because the reward will be worth the risk. So, here's the offer, and please don't get insulted, because once you factor in the money you can earn with endorsements, it really isn't too bad. Joey, we are prepared to pay you one million dollars a year. What do you say?

Joey: Man, that's a lot of money, but I just don't know. Maybe I should stay and finish high school. I'll be a senior in a couple of years and I'm kind of looking forward to the prom.

Sam: Playing hard to get, huh? I can understand that, but I'm afraid the offer is the best I can make considering your qualifications. If only there was something else you could bring to the table.

Joey: Well, I do have a tattoo on each leg and I'm planning on getting another one on my forehead.

Sam: What? Why didn't you tell me this before? That's terrific stuff. The NBA loves tattoos and they love potential. Joey, now that I know about the tattoos, I can add a half million dollars to the offer. And I'll tell you what, since we really need a wide body next year, if you can get me Fat Freddy, I'll double the offer.

There you have it, the opportunity that now exists in the wonderful world of professional sports. As Marlon Brando bemoaned in *On the Water Front,* "I coulda been a contender!" Well, in today's society, just being a contender can make for a very comfortable living. Winning is not everything, especially when just having a chance at winning pays so well!

Parents, it's not too late. Go to your kids' rooms right now and snatch those textbooks away and replace them with a ball or some sort of sports apparatus. Your kids just might be contenders.

Tell Me Who Won, I'll Tell You My Team

I recently attended my first meeting of FRA. As is the practice at such meetings, I introduced myself by saying, "Hello, my name is Roger and I am a front-runner." I then went on to tell my story. I explained how difficult it was for me to discuss sports with my buddies because our conversations always ended up with everyone pointing a finger at me and saying that I didn't have any sense of loyalty, that I only supported winners. The venom in their comments would have made a cobra proud.

During my remarks, everyone at the FRA meeting nodded in agreement with all that I said. I was definitely preaching to the choir. Every member of Front-Runners Anonymous had felt the scorn I had to endure whenever I announced that the team I was rooting for in the upcoming season happened to be the defending champions from the last season. That's what front-runners do. We pull for winners because rooting for losers seems to be a total waste of energy, but we pay a price for our rather sensible behavior.

But before I go any further, let me explain that my front-runner status only applies to professional sports. I certainly appreciate the concept of loyalty when it comes to the teams at my high school and the teams at the college I attended. Whether the teams from my alma maters are good or bad, I will always support them.

Actually, I had a high school chemistry teacher and a college Spanish professor who tried very hard to keep me from having any kind of alma mater, but I did make it in both cases and I still maintain a fierce allegiance to both schools, despite those aforementioned teachers. And because of my allegiance, when those teams win, they played great, but when they lose, the reasons for the loss are many, all of which eventually come down to horrible officiating.

My point here is that I do indeed know how to be loyal under the proper circumstances. But when it comes to professional sports, all bets are off. At the professional level, being loyal has different rules.

I get it that people who live in a state with a professional team will support the team from their state. It's like having a presidential candidate from your state. The guy may be a jerk, but he's your jerk. Even though presidential candidates may lose an election by a landslide, they always seem to carry their home state. The Pointer Sisters explained this phenomenon quite well in their hit record *We Are Family*.

For many people, this notion of family applies quite well to professional sports. The attitude is that if the home team has a miserable season, it is still the home team. Every member of the team is accepted as family and people are more willing to forgive family when they don't exactly perform as they are expected to perform. It is this spirit of forgiveness that causes people to always look to next year, or in the case of Chicago Cubs fans, the next decade.

In my case, the whole we-are-family scenario doesn't work in professional sports. The reason quite simply is that the state where I now live does not have any type of professional sports team. And the state where I was born and grew up does not have a professional team. Because of this fact, I feel that I am clearly free of any familial restraints and therefore I can darn well pull for any team. Furthermore, and most importantly, I can change my support if the team I chose does not perform very well.

Despite the fact that I do not have any residential allegiance to a pro team, my friends still insist that I should pick a team and stick with it. My answer to their request is rather simple. I tell them I will do so when the players on professional teams choose to exhibit the same degree of loyalty. At present, such player loyalty doesn't seem to exist within any professional franchise.

Where is the loyalty when some player decides to abandon his team because some other franchise is willing to pay him more money? Does this player feel any sort of obligation to the thousands of fans who shelled out big bucks to buy replicas of his jersey? Does he feel an obligation to the fans who mortgaged their home or sold their car in order to buy a pair of the sneakers their favorite player endorsed? Will the player return the money those fans spent? Will he pay for them to get the replica of the jersey he will wear for his new team? Let me help you. The answers are *no, no, no* and *no*. In case I miscounted the questions, *no*.

The fact that players are willing to follow the money is at the heart of my desire to be a front-runner. First of all, please understand that I totally understand that players would want to go to the team that will pay them the most. They usually have families to support and their careers won't last forever, so I certainly appreciate it that they want to make as much money as they can while they can.

But because of the desire to go where the money is, a team's roster can often change from year to year. And this point doesn't even take into consideration the roster changes that come about because some players want to be traded to better teams. The point is that regardless of the reasons, and actually there are many, the make-up of a team changes, and oftentimes rather dramatically, from one season to the next. Consequently, as soon as a fan gets attached to particular players, bam, those players' names no longer appear in the program.

For many fans, this circumstance does not pose a problem. These fans apparently are not concerned about the individual names that might appear on the back of a jersey. Such people believe that a Laker is a Laker, a Yankee is a Yankee, and a Steeler is a Steeler. For myself, all of the roster changes do create a problem.

The fact of the matter is that in professional sports, I pull for people, not logos or nicknames or mascots or cheerleaders. Well, it's possible cheerleaders might enter into the equation. Anyway, as a young boy, I was a Willie Mays fan. I liked him because he was a fantastic baseball player, not because he was a member of the New

York Giants. Even when he became a San Francisco Giant, it didn't matter to me. I was living in a small town in Iowa and while I didn't know where New York or San Francisco was, I did know Willie Mays could play baseball.

By the way, where was the loyalty when the Giants moved from New York to San Francisco? The whole team moved from New York to San Francisco and I'm pretty sure the owner didn't ask the fans in New York how they felt about the move. And how about when the Colts were moved in the dead of the night from Baltimore to Indianapolis? I'm positive the fans were not consulted in that move. It's bad enough when an individual player goes to another team, but when an owner abandons the fans of one city to go to another city, then the question of fan loyalty becomes a moot point.

I clearly am a sports fan. I truly enjoy athletic competitions. I've seen the thrill of victory and the agony of defeat, and I can tell you I much prefer the thrill of victory. If I'm going to devote a lot of my time to watching sports, and I am, I don't see the charm in pulling for teams more likely to offer me the agony of defeat. Losing depresses me. Winning makes me happy.

So, if people want to pull for teams from their city or state even though those teams consist of thug players who spend most of their time in bars, pampered stars who actually think there is an "i" in team, and owners who refuse to spend the money necessary to get a competitive roster, all of which lead to defeat after defeat, then go for it. Paint your bodies in the team colors, wear the jerseys and hats, buy the beer mugs with the team logo, name your kids after the coach or star player, do whatever you want to do.

For myself, I will continue to follow the team that wins the World Series or the NBA Championship or the Super Bowl. Those teams will be my teams, as long as they have players I like and they continue to win. Yes, I am a front-runner, but my teams always make the playoffs and I sleep well at night.

Section Three – Naked Women

You guessed it, this section has absolutely nothing to do with naked women. Furthermore, this section contains only words and there aren't any pictures of women, naked or clothed. The name of this chapter is clearly a blatant attempt to get my buddies to buy the book. Normally, they are not readers, although many of them say they buy *Playboy* for the articles.

Anyway, this section is really about politics, so my buddies will be sorely disappointed because they rarely discuss politics, unless some politician gets caught having some sleazy affair. Now that I think about it, my buddies talk about politics a lot.

How a Bill Becomes a Law

Even though I really did try to pay attention to everything my teacher said in my high school government class, I must confess that I never did fully understand the part about the legislative process. I suppose I might have spent a little too much time staring at one or two of the girls in my class, or maybe it was all of the girls, but the fact is that how a bill becomes a law remained a deep, dark mystery to me for a very long time. Whenever I tried to follow the process used by Congress to make laws, I ended up feeling confused, frustrated, and more nauseous than the winner of a pickled pig's feet eating contest.

I truly felt my bewilderment about the legislative process might lessen after the C-Span network created one of the first TV reality programs when it began televising Congress in action. Instead of gaining a greater insight into the workings of Congress, the only thing I learned was that the words "Congress" and "action" should never be used in the same sentence.

It was rather disconcerting when I first tuned in and saw that when the cameras spanned the chambers of either the House or the Senate, those chambers were pretty much empty. If Congress were a Broadway play, it would have closed after the first night. So, instead of continuing to watch C-Span and increasing my frustration, I began doing more extensive research on my own. I read and studied and read some more.

I truly think my diligence paid off and I now feel that I have a much better sense of the legislative process. In fact, I honestly believe I can now explain just how a bill does become a law. So here goes.

First of all, a member of Congress introduces a bill for consideration. The member will go on to explain that if the bill is passed, it will correct some highly complex, troublesome, threatening, alarming, and life-changing situation that has made every American citizen's very existence completely unbearable. In reality, it turns out that the bill actually deals with some local matter that will help the legislator get re-elected.

These bills that are created with the goal of re-election in mind are often called *pork* by political pundits and any person waging a campaign against the incumbent who introduced the bill. In public, even incumbents brand such specialized bills presented by their colleagues as pork. But in private, all members of Congress know those little pieces of bacon are the necessary largesse needed to retain their seats and the really great health care plan that comes with it.

Legislators have long realized that bringing home the bacon is actually bringing home the votes. In point of fact, the system clearly works since incumbents usually win elections. Apparently there are large numbers of taxpayers out there who don't have any objections to the process of distributing pork as long as the bacon is fried in their pan.

Perhaps the procedure for coming up with an issue, writing a bill, and then passing it into law can best be understood by looking at how Sen. Needavote recently handled the matter. The good Senator was deeply involved in his campaign for re-election, a situation that apparently begins for all legislators right after they take their oath of office. Consequently, he had to give the voters in his state a good reason for sending him back to the Senate.

It was important that the Senator show the home folks that he had been hard at work in Washington, despite those forty-seven times he missed a vote because he was on fact-finding missions in the Bahamas or Aruba or any Caribbean island he thought might be on the verge of building a nuclear weapon. Sen. Needavote always explained his junkets by standing in front of an American flag and pointing out that his number one priority was to keep America safe and he would travel wherever necessary to achieve that end. Besides keeping the islands clear of nuclear weapons, the Senator managed to get the best tan of anyone in the Senate.

In trying to think of an issue for his bill that would best help his constituency, Sen. Needavote remembered that when he was a child, his beloved mother always warned him about the dangers of running with scissors. Suddenly bells went off in his head, not the loud bells found in the steeple of a large church, but the whimpering tinkles of a traveler's alarm clock with the batteries running low. Members of Congress rarely hear loud bells.

The senator reasoned that offering a bill making it illegal for children to run with scissors would make him a hero, especially to mothers, but also to all voters who were concerned about children. While bills that offer protection to people for just about anything will usually garner public support, protecting children is a guaranteed vote getter.

While the bill would give the senator the votes of every mother in his state, he would gain even greater support from voters because of the money the bill would bring to the state. He had actually thought everything out quite well. First of all, a key component of his running-with-scissors bill called for the construction of a research facility where studies would be conducted to establish once and for all that the warning mothers had been giving for generations was indeed valid. If running with scissors was dangerous, scientific research would prove it. Of course, the multimillion dollar facility would be built in his state.

To avoid the critics who might label the expensive research facility as being too limited in scope, Sen. Needavote pointed out that the research lab would actually study the dangers of running with any sharp objects, not just scissors. Objects to be studied included such things as machetes and incorrectly closed safety pins. And furthermore, the senator stated that while protecting children was his number one priority, he noted that the facility would also be able to research the dangers experienced by adults who run with sharp objects.

While Senator Needavote's bill was already extremely expensive, the cost overruns doubled the final price tag. Such a costly bill actually is just the kind members of Congress prefer. If a bill doesn't end up costing zillions, the fear of the bill's sponsor is that it will be perceived by other legislators as not being all that important. And while zillions added to the deficit may appear to be a bad thing to many people, it isn't regarded in that light by members of Congress if it brings jobs to a senator's state or a congressman's district. Remember, pork is just fine if it is cooked in the right kitchen.

Now, once Senator Needavote offered his bill, he had to get his colleagues' support. Presenting a bill is not enough. Passage of the bill is crucial if the home folks are really going to be happy. Trying to help people is admirable, but actually helping certain voters is imperative. Sen. Needavote didn't want a Humanitarian of the Year Award, he wanted to be re-elected to Congress. The point being that humanitarians don't get the wonderful perks that members of Congress get.

Getting the necessary votes from colleagues involves a procedure that at the Constitutional Convention was called "compromise," but today it is simply called "you-scratch-my-back-I'll-scratch-yours." In days gone by, compromise was used to accomplish something on a grand scale, something that would benefit many people. Today's politicians really don't do things on a grand scale. They just want to help registered voters in their state or district, large campaign contributors, and beloved aunts and uncles.

Sen. Needavote used the "you-scratch-my-back-I'll-scratch-yours" technique to get support for his bill. His technique was rather simple and quite common. If other senators would vote for his bill, he made it clear he would gladly support their pending pieces of legislation, everything from a bill calling for the construction of eleven ice cube factories in Alaska to a bill authorizing a study of the sex life of the blue-breasted, yellow-winged, curly-headed, but slightly balding, chickadee. He even said he would vote for the study to determine if there actually were such birds as blue-breasted, yellow-winged, curly-headed, but slightly balding, chickadees.

Actually, the chickadee project already had plenty of support because it involved junkets to Las Vegas and Miami, the only two places where the bird was ever reported to have been seen. No one knew who made the reports and not one congressperson ever asked.

Deal making is essential to the passage of any bill. And the fact of the matter is that many of the deals that are made would please used car salesmen and guys peddling Rolex watches on street corners in New York City. How else would the bill calling for the construction of the infamous "bridge to nowhere" in Alaska have ever been passed?

Okay, let me summarize the steps of how a bill becomes a law. Members of Congress come up with bills that will help them get re-elected. Colleagues support each other's bills so they all can get re-elected. Such bills only help isolated segments of the population. These bills become law. Far-reaching bills that would affect the entire country are debated, filibustered, tabled, or whatever is necessary to avoid having to vote on them. These bills rarely become laws. Any questions?

What's in a Name?

Shakespeare may have been the first to point out that names of things really do not matter, only what things are. And he made his point quite nicely in Romeo and Juliet.

> What's in a name? That which we call a rose
> By any other name would still smell as sweet.

Seemingly it would be rather difficult to dispute his logic. Not so fast there, bucko. Members of Congress apparently are not fans of Shakespeare, or even readers of the Bard, for that matter. Our duly elected lawmakers do in fact see great purpose in names, so much so they have a rule that all bills must have a number and an official title.

While the numbering part doesn't present much of a problem, the naming part has now become an important partisan ploy to obtain votes for a particular piece of legislation. In days gone by, when legislators were satisfied to let the content of a bill speak for itself, the names of bills were straightforward. Bills were given such titles as the Civil Rights Act, The Homestead Act, and the Highway Beautification Act.

The names were neutral, giving little insight as to the content of the bill. If a member of Congress was going to have a position when the debate began concerning the passage or rejection of the bill, the bill would have to be read.

Such is no longer the case. Titles of bills are now most often geared to alert party members, and both Democrats and Republicans play this game, as to whether or not they should be for or against the bill. This bit of information is extremely helpful because it allows members to take a position without having to read the bill. After all, members of Congress have extremely busy schedules as they seem to always be in re-election mode and that entails a lot of campaign-type activities. Reading and understanding particular pieces of legislation is down pretty low on their things-to-do list.

Witness some recent titles of bills that have been introduced in Congress. There is the Reducing Barack Obama's Unsustainable Deficit Act, the Big Oil Welfare Repeal Act, Repealing the Job-Killing Health Care Law Act, the Reversing President Obama's Offshore Moratorium Act, and the Repealing Ineffective and Incomplete Abstinence-Only Program Funding Act. The names of these bills make it pretty obvious if the bill is to get Democratic or Republican support even without really knowing the details of what is in the bill.

What's in a name? Apparently a great deal.

A somewhat different tactic is employed in the acronyms given to bills. (Evidently saying the actual title of a bill is also too time-consuming.) The purpose for using acronyms is that they will garner votes from both parties by the acronym alone. They don't always succeed, but they definitely would cause a lawmaker to think twice before voting against the bill. That alone would be quite an accomplishment since it is questionable that members of Congress think once, let alone twice, before doing anything.

Let me give a few examples, and all of these were or are actual bills in Congress. One such bill that might be difficult to be against is HIRE—Hiring Incentives to Restore Employment. Even without knowing exactly what the bill contains, who wants to go on record in this economy as having voted against a bill called the HIRE Act?

And then there is DREAM—Development, Relief and Education for Alien Minors. While the content of the bill might not appeal to both parties, it would take some fast talking to explain to voters why a congressman didn't support the DREAM Act. Members of Congress are often accused of taking things from voters, but our dreams? That would be a tough sell.

How about the HAPPY Act—Humanity and Pets Partnering

through the Years Act. Granted, not everyone is a pet lover, but can you imagine standing on the steps of Congress to announce that you were going to vote against the HAPPY Act? It might be best for members of Congress to vote against this bill in the dead of the night, like they do when they vote for a pay raise.

Sometimes a bill and its acronym seem to defy the real purpose of Congress. Did anyone ever hear of the BOSS ACT? This acronym for Bruce Springsteen's nickname was introduced to overhaul the concert ticket industry and improve fans' chances of scoring tickets to their favorite acts. Thank you, Congress. Now how about introducing a bill called the Garner Energy To Make Employment Always Just On Board, better know as Get Me a Job.

On occasion there are acronyms used for bills that not only defy the real purpose of Congress, they defy logic. There was the case of the congressman who wanted to name a bill after his wife, Lu. I'm not sure if his gesture was to be an anniversary present or an apology for something he did wrong. Anyway, he gave the task to his staff. Quite possibly after several drinks at some D.C. pub, the staff came up with The Transportation Equity Act: A Legacy for Users. The acronym was TEA-LU.

The irony is that after going to the trouble of creating complicated names and clever acronyms for bills, of the thousands of them that are introduced in Congress each year, only about three percent become law. If basketball players had that kind of shooting percentage or baseball leadoff hitters had that kind of batting average, they would be looking for work. But despite the low production rate, members of Congress continue to receive a good salary and a great pension. There doesn't seem to be much incentive for them to increase their rate of production. Based on some of the bills they come up with, that's just as well!

It makes one wonder, how much wood would a woodchuck chuck if a woodchuck worked for Congress? What is a woodchuck anyway? Some call the animal a groundhog, some a whistle-pig, and still others, a land-beaver. Does it really matter? What's in a name anyway? Well, apparently to Congress, a great deal.

When in Doubt, Take a Poll

In the United States we have a representative democracy. We elect our leaders and they are to represent us in running the country. In theory, this relationship would imply that those elected leaders would carry out the wishes of the electorate.

Herein lies a bit of a quandary. How are the elected representatives to discover just what it is that the people want done? Perhaps James Madison, the Father of the Constitution, offered the best solution to this problem when he said after the convention where he got his nickname, "Gentlemen, what in the hell do we do now? I say we poll the people. My Uncle Gallup will help."

Since this suggestion ignored the fact that prior to and during the writing of the Constitution, the people were pretty much left out of the process, the rest of the forefathers just rolled their eyes and replied, "Yeah, whatever." Then all of the delegates went to a tavern.

As it has turned out, Madison's suggestion about elected officials using polls to ascertain the wishes of their constituents has indeed evolved in a most interesting fashion. Actually, it is somewhat remarkable that the suggestion still exists since members of Congress today don't seem particularly concerned about ascertaining the wishes of their constituents, unless said constituents make really, really big campaign contributions, or they work as lobbyists for groups that make really, really big campaign contributions.

The lack of concern by members of Congress for discovering the wishes of the voters who don't have deep pockets primarily exists because dealing with those who do have deep pockets is rather time-consuming. There are all of those fact-finding meetings on the ski slopes of Vail or on the beaches in Miami. That doesn't leave much time to find out what the common voters want. By common voters, I mean the people who don't get invited to ski in Vail or sunbathe in Miami.

In order to tap into the wishes of the common voters, the utility of Madison's suggestion about polling has taken on some significance. While unmarked bills in unmarked envelopes stuck in a politician's unmarked pocket certainly relay the message of how these voters who have a lot of unmarked bills want an elected official to vote on a particular issue, such transactions do not tell the politicians what the common voters want to happen concerning the same issue.

But since elected officials need to be elected, they realize they must at least pretend to have some degree of interest in the views of their constituents who don't vote with their checkbooks, but who do indeed vote. On occasion, they even vote in numbers large enough to actually make a difference in an election's outcome. It turns out that polling is a really good way to ascertain just what the wishes of these voters might be. This information can be most helpful, especially if it doesn't run contrary to the big bucks constituents.

Reliance on the polling process has become so important, pollsters, hundreds and hundreds of pollsters, are now a vital part of every politician's staff. These inquisitive folks, all of whom can probably trace their roots to Madison's Uncle Gallup, are truly committed to discovering the likes and dislikes, hopes and fears, wants and needs, and sexual behaviors of every American citizen, data which can be useful in helping a particular official know his or her position on numbers of issues.

While there are numerous polls being taken nowadays, political polls seem to receive the most attention, particularly in an election year, and some elected official somewhere is up for re-election every year. Even though the political polls purport to show what the common voters want, the politicians have discovered the wishes of these voters often run contrary to the wishes of their big-spending voters. Not surprisingly, politicians have found a way to solve this seeming predicament.

To understand this solution, one needs to examine how poll data is used. First of all, the data from political polls generally is used by elected officials to explain their position on any given issue. The explanations take the form of *talking points*. Talking points are a good thing because politicians, if nothing else and there really is nothing else, do indeed love to talk. To put it simply, since we are dealing with politicians here, talking points are a list of generalities used in speeches and interviews because specifics are apparently way too confusing for them to grasp.

Since political polling is often done by the politicians themselves (remember all of those pollsters on the payroll?), the results should raise eyebrows. While the results of any poll can be affected by things like the number and make-up of respondents, the wording of the questions, and the mysterious margin of error, these factors frequently are manipulated. Apparently this situation exists because it is imperative that the results of political polls reflect the agenda of the politician.

To guarantee the data generated from a poll supports a politician's position, it is important that the poll be completed in a specific way. Step one in this process is choosing the right number and make-up of respondents. For example, if a politician would like to see gambling come to his state, a poll conducted among the membership of the blackjack dealers union most certainly would provide the necessary data. And if some politician is in favor of legalizing drugs, polling the "Chainsaw Termite" and the "Butt-Kickin Bubba Boy" rock bands and all of their fans would no doubt deliver the favorable numbers to show support for drug legalization.

When announcing the results that "Eighty-seven percent of the voters favor gambling," or "Ninety-three percent of the voters favor the legalization of drugs," politicians never see the necessity of divulging the number and make-up of the respondents. If asked about the absence of such details, the response is an assurance to everyone that an aide will provide that information at a later date. In political speak, "later" means that the information will be available when every American citizen has the same health care coverage as members of Congress, or elected officials stop being influenced by people who make really, really big campaign contributions. Don't hold your breath for either contingency to occur.

The wording used on poll questions can also skew the results in the direction the politician needs. If incumbent Senator Crabgrass, a crafty old politician, wants data to show that he is leading his opponent, Nick Newboy, he will just have his pollster take a carefully worded poll. The poll will consist of two questions. Question one: "Will you vote for Nick Newboy if it turns out he smokes crack while stealing canned goods from a charity food bank?" Question two: "Will you vote for Sen. Crabgrass, a man who fights drug gangs and gives food to charity food banks?" How people answer those questions is pretty obvious, and the results will bring the necessary headline: "SENATOR CRABGRASS OVERWHELMING FAVORITE OVER OPPONENT."

Of all of the quirks of polls, the *margin of error* issue is perhaps the most confusing. Every poll has one and the margin differs from poll to poll. The reason for the difference is because of a complex formula involving the number of respondents, astrology, and the circumference of a pan pizza with anchovies. At least I think that is the formula. The size of this *margin of error* affects how the poll results should be interpreted.

Some may ask, "Why is there even such a thing as a *margin of error?*" Evidently it exists because the number of respondents differs from poll to poll, but more importantly, because of the fact that people who are asked questions about earthshaking issues sometimes—how should I say this—lie through their teeth. Now this is a concept politicians can understand.

There are several reasons why some people do not tell the truth when being polled: 1) the respondent has no opinion, but is too embarrassed to let anyone know, so he makes one up; 2) the respondent does have an opinion, but doesn't think it's anyone's business, so he fabricates another viewpoint; 3) the respondent suffers from pollitis, which is an uncontrollable urge to lie to people who ask questions about earthshaking issues; and finally, 4) the respondent just likes to mess with people's minds.

We are now back to the original quandary. If the way politicians use poll data cannot be trusted, how can the little people be heard? It seems apparent that Madison's plea to "poll the people" (you know, maybe he really didn't say that) simply will not work.

Perhaps now is the time to follow the advice of another of the forefathers, Thomas Jefferson. He once said, while having a few brews with the boys at a popular Philadelphia tavern, "Yo, dudes, maybe we should just get a Facebook account and communicate with the people that way." Naw, that wouldn't work either. Facebook relies on friends, and politicians have so few, unless they make really, really big campaign contributions.

After winning a tremendous upset victory in the American Revolution, a conflict in which bookies in London had the Colonies as a 10 to 1 underdog, the upstart nation quickly realized it was in a kind of "be-careful-what-you-wish-for" situation. The leaders of the Colonies, who became known as the Forefathers, realized they would now have to actually create their own government. The problem was that no one was sure what form that government should actually take.

It was decided to have a meeting in Philadelphia in the heat of the summer, nail the windows shut in the building where the meeting would be held, and hatch out a plan. That meeting produced the Constitution of the United States. Who knew that sweating men in wigs could do such good work?

An important part of the process in creating the government was to determine what type of leader should be at the top. After having just waged the Revolution to overthrow a tyrannical king, it seemed to be a no-brainer that having a monarch was not a serious option. The only condition that would have possibly allowed the new country to be led by a king, but not the tyrannical kind, was if George Washington, clearly the most popular man in the Colonies at this time, would have agreed to become king.

Although he was offered the position, Washington didn't have any interest in the king gig, so the Forefathers created the position of president. The presidency did pique Old George's interest. He somehow knew that the dental plan for a president would be better than the dental plan for a king, much the same way he knew standing up in a boat would make a great painting.

As it turned out, the good dental plan actually became a crackerjack health care plan in general. The plan turned out to be so good, every president, and even every member of Congress since, have become enamored with the medical coverage the plan provides for elected officials.

They are so enamored that whenever there is talk about what programs to cut in order to fight the deficit problem facing the country, no one in Congress or the Oval Office ever suggests cutting the health care plan of elected officials in D.C. as an important first step, or any step for that matter, to deal with the huge deficit. Apparently having Forefathers has evolved into having "for fathers."

Anyway, while the Forefathers did a good job in organizing the governmental structure of their new country, they did make one glaring mistake concerning the presidency, not counting that messy electoral college thing. The mistake is that they didn't provide any guidance for the nominating procedure and the subsequent campaigning for those folks seeking to become president. While the nominating part has become ridiculously complicated, the campaigning part has become utterly disgraceful, and unfortunately, always the twain shall meet.

For the most part, the lack of guidance has led presidential campaigns today to become petty, befuddling, lacking in intelligence, and in terms of giving voters any significant information as to why to vote for a particular candidate, they are completely devoid of any merit whatsoever. Maybe I sugarcoated that a bit, but the point is that since the Forefathers did not provide the slightest hint as to the best way for candidates to convince voters why they should receive their votes, presidential campaigning today is, and I want to be fair here, nauseating.

The first step of any campaign for the presidency, and this is crucial, is to start holding fundraisers in order to raise the fifty bazillion dollars, and some loose change, needed to make a legitimate run for the office. As obscene as the money-raising part of this process happens to be, it all goes downhill from there.

While there were certainly some irksome campaign methods that were used in the early days of presidential campaigning, they clearly were not as annoying as the methods used today. A particularly distressing part of present campaigns is the reliance on overtly negative thirty-second TV ads that give support to a particular candidate only by condemning and criticizing the opponent. The logic behind the ads is to convince people that Smith is such a low-life scum, voters should therefore vote for Jones primarily because he is not Smith, who by the way happens to be a low-life scum.

The obnoxious ads are most often paid for by super PACs. These mysterious political action committees can basically conceal the identity of the donors who end up contributing a large portion of the aforementioned fifty bazillion dollars, and some loose change, needed to run a campaign. The fact that these political ATMs exist provides a shield for the candidates. Since a candidate's official campaign organization legally is to be separate from the super PACs, wink, wink, those PACs can make ads containing vicious negative attacks and the candidate himself doesn't have to say "I approve of this message."

This "I-know-nothing" technique allows the candidate to stand above the fray and come across as a nice guy who doesn't delve into dirty politics, not that anyone thinks politicians ever delve into dirty politics.

Another problem with present-day campaigns are the campaign speeches. Actually, "speeches" is a misnomer because for the most part there really is only one speech. While that has always been the case, the problem "one speech" creates is more magnified today. The reason for this situation is that today's technology has made having one speech much, much more problematic.

While presidential candidates have always traveled around the country when campaigning, in days gone by the lack of speedy communication allowed a candidate to deliver the same speech, now referred to as the stump speech, in town after town and no one was the wiser. Today, though, the speed with which the news media and the social media spread information is astounding. Unfortunately, politicians seem oblivious to this fact, and many other facts for that matter.

This clueless state of most candidates does create a bit of a problem. The candidates out on the campaign trail today assume that the people at each of their many stops do not watch TV, listen to the radio, read a newspaper, own a computer, or have a cell phone. They don't seem to realize that by the time they go from one town to the next, their previous speech has been reported in the newspaper, aired on the radio, and shown on TV, with every word being dissected and analyzed ad nauseam. And, trust me, the news media is really good at "ad nauseam."

Because of their apparent lack of understanding concerning the extensive coverage their speeches get, the candidates go ahead and deliver the same speech in city after city as if they were expressing prudent ideas to their listeners for the first time. The result is that the already pretty awful speech now becomes boringly repetitive.

While the aforementioned reasons explain why presidential campaigns today are annoying, troublesome, and lacking in substance, the epitome of exasperation concerning campaigns occurs when the candidates debate. By debate, I am not referring to any sort of political discourse that would even be remotely recognized by either Lincoln or Douglas, but a form of discussion that allows only two or three minute responses to questions that require much more. Thank you, TV networks, for fostering such a troublesome format.

The two or three minutes given to the candidates doesn't allow them enough time to explain positions on how to end the deficit, lower gas prices, or end wars. And the format certainly doesn't give them enough time to explain their reluctance to produce their tax returns, clear up why they keep their secretary at work overnight every weekend, and defend their use of marijuana when they were teenagers, college students, or when Willie Nelson visited their house last week.

To be quite honest, as imperfect as this debate format appears, it probably does have its supporters in a society that possesses an attention span that lasts as long as it takes to type typical responses on Twitter or Facebook, such as "Smith U rock" or "Jones is my BFF." And of course, if a candidate says something out of the ordinary, there will be the classic "LOL" or "OMG." It's not always clear if those particular shorthand text responses are positive or negative, but texting doesn't exactly allow for definitive explanations any more than the debate format itself.

What is quite interesting about presidential debates, as flawed as they happen to be, is the fact that there is not a shortage of organizations willing to sponsor the verbal jousting matches that now pass as debates. On the local level, there are civic groups such as the League of Women Voters and the Beer Drinking Boys of Big Betty's Bar and Grill that are more than willing to step forward. These and many other such civic groups feel it is extremely important for voters to know where each of the candidates stand on some of the important issues of the day, and all of the trivial ones.

On the national level, where the presidential candidates are most likely to battle, the debates are usually sponsored by the TV networks. The networks often take the high road and explain their sponsorship of the debates as yet another step in their continuing quest to preserve democracy, which doesn't exactly explain why programs like "Kim Kardashian Offers Advice to Demi Moore" or "Oprah Interviews Oprah" make the airwaves on their network. The "preserving democracy" ploy certainly sounds more noble than saying the debates are being presented tonight because the women of *The Real Housewives of Topeka* need a break in order to receive counseling, to have plastic surgery involving the wearing of bigger bras, and to take IQ tests.

Perhaps the most disturbing part of the debates is not in what is asked and what is answered, but in how the network analysts interpret what has been said. For example, it always appears that Fox and MSNBC attend a different debate, even though the debate they are analyzing occurred at the same time in the same place. Apparently, networks are as concerned with political spin as are the candidates. Instead of being news, the debates are actually political opportunities for the networks as well as for the candidates.

While presidential campaigns are supposed to be informative and essential events in preserving our democracy, they actually are hazardous to the health of every voter in America. While the Constitution does guarantee the right to vote, perhaps it also needs to guarantee freedom from the obnoxious behavior leading up to that vote, i.e., political campaigns. This behavior can definitely cause the voters a lot of headaches, upset stomachs, and an uncontrollable urge to lock themselves in a closet and scream.

Now if the voters had a good health care plan like the president's, they could have all of those problems treated for little cost to themselves. The problem is that to get that kind of coverage, you need to be elected president. To be elected president, you need to campaign. To campaign, you need to—oh, never mind.

When a presidential election is over in the United States, everyone usually feels a tremendous amount of relief, regardless of whether or not their candidate came out as the winner. The circumstance that leads to such an attitude is that campaigns nowadays last so very long. People finally reach a point where they just want them to be over. It's only possible to endure but so many speeches full of empty promises, negative thirty-second ads, meaningless debates, campaign posters littering roads, and editorials detailing why John Doe is better than Betty Buck. And furthermore, everyone knows that once the last vote is counted, there will be just two or three days before the next campaign begins. Everyone needs a break, even a tiny break.

Another concern with presidential elections, besides the length of the campaigns, is that it seems that each year there are more and more voters who don't feel comfortable with any of the candidates. Invariably, there are extremely large numbers of voters who feel they are simply voting for the lesser of two evils.

Perhaps there is a bit of validity in that position. Maybe the best people simply do not choose to run for office. It is indeed quite possible that there are many extremely qualified people who don't run for any office because they don't want to face the media scrutiny that entails endless questions that really seem to have little to do with a person's qualifications to be a senator or governor or president or whatever.

It is quite possible that holding a public office has become too public for some people, and consequently there are some outstanding potential candidates who choose to remain on the sidelines to avoid overzealous reporters whose questions are more prying than pertinent.

Take the case of a man who probably would be the perfect candidate for the presidency. He is a very beloved humanitarian who truly believes in giving to rich and poor alike. He is a man who has traveled to the far corners of the world and is always greeted with open arms.

I am, of course, speaking of Santa Claus. Unfortunately, even though he has numerous excellent qualifications, he has never considered running for the presidency. His reasons for staying on the sidelines are rather simple. Santa doesn't want to deal with those relentless members of the media who evidently see their job as making the news rather than reporting it. Such reporters enjoy creating controversy far more than simply reporting what a candidate has to say on a given issue. Santa is too nice of a man to have to endure what the media would throw at him during a press conference.

Santa: Ho! Ho! Ho! Good afternoon, ladies and gentlemen. It's great to see all of you again. As usual, I have a very busy schedule, so let's get right to your questions.

1st reporter: It's been reported that you are making a list, checking it twice, trying to find out who is naughty or nice. Santa, are you spying on people? Are you violating their right to privacy? What do you plan to do with this list?

Santa: Well, yes, I do have a list, but it's necessary to do my job. It's all perfectly harmless. I don't spy on anyone. The information I use to compile my list is given to me voluntarily. People write me letters telling me the things I need to know.

1st reporter: Yeah, sure, whatever. Are you going to make this list public?

Santa: Ho! Ho! Ho! Oh no, I can't do that. I am given the information in strict confidence. It is not for public consumption.

1st reporter: Are you going to tell us your sources? If not, what are you hiding?

Santa: Ho! Ho! Ho! I'm not hiding anything. What are you hiding when you print information that is attributed to "unnamed sources"?

1st reporter: We ask the questions here! You just answer the questions.

2nd reporter: Santa, if I might change the subject. I want to ask you about the happiness issue.

Santa: The happiness issue? What are you talking about? I don't understand what you mean.

2nd reporter: You know what I mean, Santa. I'm talking about all of your "ho, ho, ho" stuff. It seems rather strange that a guy who works as long and as hard as you do could always go around being so happy. You are too jolly, Santa. That just isn't natural.

Santa: I still don't think I get your point.

2nd reporter: Okay, Santa, I'll spell it out. Do you use drugs?

Santa: Ho! Ho! Ho! Where do you people get these questions?

2nd reporter: Quit stalling. Just answer the question.

Santa: No, I do not use drugs, although I must admit I've had opportunities. You'd be surprised at the stuff people leave for me by the chimney. It's not always cookies and milk. Ho! Ho! Ho!

2nd reporter: So we are to believe that you have access to all of these drugs and yet you always look the other way? Santa, the point is that you visit many, many houses where drugs are available.

Santa: But I said that…

3rd reporter: We know what you said and we'll determine what you mean. But now I want to ask you about your relationship with the big toy manufacturers. Aren't you a tool for these toy companies?

Santa: That is not true. Everyone knows my elves make all of the toys I deliver.

4th reporter: Speaking of elves, it's been reported that most of your elves do not have their green cards.

Santa: Who reported that?

4th reporter: I'm going to report it as soon as I leave this news conference. Is it true or not?

Santa: All of the elves are legal, but there are many trolls who are illegal immigrants, but I do not employ any trolls.

5th reporter: Isn't it true that you don't employ trolls because they refuse to work in the sweatshop you run? Santa, are you in violation of labor laws?

Santa: Wherever did you get that information?

5th reporter: I just thought of it. Is it true or not?

Santa: That is absurd. Look, this conference has to end. Mrs. Claus and I....

6th reporter: Are you two still together?

Santa: Excuse me? What are you talking about? Is this more information you just thought of at this very moment?

6th reporter: Come on, Santa, we all know you stopped at Jennifer Aniston's house last year.

Santa: I stop at a lot of houses.

6th reporter: Sure, but my sources report you stayed at her house longer than your usual stops. Come on, Santa, are you and Jennifer having an affair?

Santa: Ho! Ho! Ho! I'm flattered by the insinuation of your question. At my age, it's truly a compliment for you to imply I had a fling with Jennifer Aniston, although I'm sure it won't do much for her reputation. I'd like to take more questions, but I have to leave.

6th reporter: Wait a minute, Santa, you didn't answer my question.

Santa: I know.

There you go. It's no wonder some of the best and the brightest remain on the sidelines. Skeletons in the closet or not, it is a safe bet that the media or the opposition will come up with something to try to discourage people from voting for a particular candidate, qualified or not. Heck, I probably could have been elected president if I hadn't gotten that speeding ticket on my tricycle when I was in first grade.

The Best Job in the Country

It never fails. After the last vote is counted in a presidential election, the media and people everywhere begin speculating about the next election. Even dolphins, using a highly complex series of clicks, begin discussing the potential candidates for the race to be held four years in the future. The opinions offered by the media and fed to the people are pretty much senseless drivel, but the dolphins usually make some very pertinent observations.

The point is that there is an American obsession with the office of the president of the United States. While this obsession is not always expressed by people actually taking time to vote in presidential elections, there is no shortage of talk about the person who happens to hold the job and the folks who yearn for that job. Without such discussions there wouldn't be taverns, barbershops and Sunday morning talk shows.

I find the situation most perplexing. The fact of the matter is that the job of president is the most difficult job in the world, and the pay really isn't very good. Third-string quarterbacks in the NFL make much more money than the President. And yet, there is always a long line of people seeking the presidency, and untold numbers of people who are more than willing to tell whoever holds the job how it should be done.

I just don't get it. To be quite honest, I have never seen the charm of being president, even with the perks, and there are some truly neat perks. Who would complain about having people who will cook and clean for you, walk your dog, take out the trash, cut the grass, and drive or fly you wherever you want to go? And how cool is it that when you are in a car, you never have to stop at a red light? And if you'd rather fly, in your own plane by the way, you don't have to take your shoes off before boarding. While those things are indeed rather appealing on one level, because of the many responsibilities, I still find the job much too stressful.

Being president just never caught my fancy. Even as a child I wasn't thrilled when my parents said I could grow up to be president. Actually, I was a bit hurt that they had apparently underestimated my intelligence. Despite my young age, I still realized there was a much better job out there. I wanted that job then and I still do. In fact, I am now ready to make my childhood, and adulthood, dream come true. I now want to declare my candidacy to become the vice president of the United States, which happens to be the best job in the country.

I originally planned to make my declaration on one of the TV news talk shows, but no one seemed interested, not *Hannity* or *Meet the Press* or *Face the Nation*. Neither *The View* nor *Rush* offered me time on their shows. *Entertainment Tonight* didn't want to touch the story unless I had partied with Charlie Sheen or dated Lady Gaga. Regardless of the snub by the mainstream media, I remain undaunted. If Bill O'Reilly or Chris Mathews didn't want to interview me about my candidacy for the greatest job in the world, then I knew I would just have to interview myself.

Reporter Loring: Okay, what's the story here? I have a busy schedule, so let's get on with it. I'm supposed to interview some guy who has invented a roach hotel that serves a free continental breakfast and has free in-room movies. He claims his hotels attract more roaches that way. Cool, huh! Anyway, what's this big political announcement you want to make? Let me guess, you're planning to run for president.

Candidate Loring: Don't be ridiculous! I'd rather eat tofu soaked in vinegar than run for president! I'm a much brighter person than that. No, today I am officially announcing my candidacy for the vice presidency of the United States of America.

Reporter Loring: Vice president? I thought you said you were a bright guy! You obviously don't know your American history. It was our first vice president, John Adams, who described his job as the "most insignificant office that ever the invention of man contrived or his imagination conceived." Not exactly a ringing endorsement, and that's the job you want? I don't think we need to stop the presses for this one! You're a whacko.

Candidate Loring: With all due respect to Mr. Adams, and none to you, he was wrong. Actually, as it has turned out, being vice president is a fantastic job. Granted, the pay is not tremendous, although $227,300 isn't that bad for the minimal workload required for the job. Granted, batboys for the Yankees make more money, but they have to work harder. And Yankee batboys don't get limos and their own plane and a house and free tickets to some really great concerts, just to name a few things that separate them from a VP.

Reporter Loring: Whoa, slow down a minute. Your concept of the vice presidency sounds pretty selfish to me. You seem to have forgotten the "public servant" part of the job. Vice presidents are supposed to serve, not take.

Candidate Loring: What planet do you live on? Let me give you a bit of an education here. Policemen are public servants. Firemen are public servants. The vice president is just a back-up for the president.

Reporter Loring: Maybe he's a back-up, but he is just a heartbeat away from the mother of all public servants—the president of the United States.

Candidate Loring: And your point is…?

Reporter Loring: My point is that while you say you like the vice president's perks, your eye is really on the prize of the presidency, the mother lode of perks. Your real motive is that you want to use the vice presidency as a stepping stone to the presidency.

Candidate Loring: Excuse me? You obviously have not been listening. Let me be a little more clear. The president's job is a thankless one. He has far too many really hard decisions to make and there are always going to be large numbers of people who will disagree with his decisions. I definitely do not want that pressure and that grief, so let me make this crystal clear: if I do become vice president and something should happen to the president, I can assure you that I will refuse to take his place. Forget the Constitution on this one. I will gladly give up my position in the line of succession, as long as I could remain as vice president. My ambition ends there. Now do you get it?

Reporter Loring: Okay, let's forget for a minute whether you would or would not become president if the opportunity presented itself. Let me take this discussion in a different direction. Just what makes you think you are even qualified to be vice president?

Candidate Loring: I'm qualified because I'm a citizen, I'm over thirty-five years of age and I've lived here over fourteen years. Are there other qualifications you are looking for?

Reporter Loring: Sure. What makes you think you are capable of doing the job? What abilities do you bring to the table?

Candidate Loring: Listen, buddy, doctors need abilities. Plumbers need abilities. Vice presidents just need to stay out of the way, unless there is a state funeral in Albania or a royal wedding in Tonga. Vice presidents are ceremonial people. They don't need to have ideas or plans or visions. They need to show up for work without anyone noticing. Look at some of our best vice presidents, men like Henry Wilson, George Dallas, Hannibal Hamlin, Levi Morton, and Jared Ingersoll.

Reporter Loring: Wait a minute, I never heard of any of those guys.

Candidate Loring: Exactly. You never heard of them because they never did anything of consequence, which was exactly their job description. Each and every one of them would be in the Vice President's Hall of Fame if it existed. A great vice president is defined by what he didn't do instead of what he did.

Reporter Loring: But a vice president is also President of the Senate. He is an advisor to the president. He's a spokesman for administration policies.

Candidate Loring: There you go again. What is your point this time?

Reporter Loring: The point is that a vice president doesn't just do ceremonial jobs. There are other responsibilities. There are meaningful things to do. For example, you realize a vice president has to break ties in the Senate, don't you?

Candidate Loring: You're a new political reporter, aren't you? Let me explain a few things. First of all, vice presidents rarely, rarely, rarely preside over the Senate. And if one of those extremely rare occasions should arise, I'm sure I could fit that task into my schedule if I had to, as long as it didn't interfere with my golf game. As far as breaking tie votes, senators don't actually vote all that much anyway. They offer a lot of bills and then they just debate them forever, debates in which the two parties blame each other for inaction. The chances for any vote on an important bill is pretty slim, but the chance for a tie vote on any bill is about as likely as either party giving the other credit for having a good idea. But if I should have to cast a tie-breaking vote, well, I'll just call in sick.

Reporter Loring: But what about those times when the president asks you for advice. Don't you feel any obligation to help your boss?

Candidate Loring: Advice? A president asking a vice president for advice? What a bizarre concept. Listen, vice presidents are not picked because they can help the president make decisions. They are picked because the Constitution requires it and the state they happen to live in might be helpful in obtaining the necessary number of electoral votes for the ticket to be elected. But once they are chosen, they are expected to stay out of sight and out of mind, unless they are needed to greet the new ambassador from Madagascar or address the annual convention of SLAR, Sexy Ladies of the American Revolution. Not every woman looked like Martha Washington, you know. Anyway, I'm telling you the job is easy and I really want it.

Reporter Loring: Well, which party are you most compatible with, Republican or Democrat? Surely your political philosophy could not work with either party.

Candidate Loring: Political philosophy? Let me try this one

more time. Vice presidents are basically nonentities. They don't need a political philosophy, although they can conjure up one if it helps their chances to be selected by a particular party. For myself, I don't care which party chooses me to be on their ticket. I can adjust my views in a heartbeat. I can be for or against big government, I can support "don't ask, don't tell," or "wow, I never thought about it." As long as I'm allowed to be vice president, I can be like a chameleon. I will be whatever I'm wanted to be. Tell me what to say, I'll say it. Tell me what to do, I'll do it. When all is said and done, then just point me to the VP's house and I'll be happy.

Reporter Loring: This interview is giving me a headache. Let me ask one more question and then I'm calling it a day. Just why do you think you deserve to be vice president of the United States?

Candidate Loring: Hey, dude, that's pretty simple. I asked first.

Just Tell Me Who Won

There was a time when the reporting of election results was quick and straight to the point. The report started with a brief interruption of whatever TV show was on at the time. A serious-looking anchorman would come on the screen. He would stare directly at the camera and say, usually in a deep, authoritative voice, "Paul Politician has 57,685 votes and Carl Candidate has 32,602 votes. We declare Paul Politician to be the winner because he has the most votes. We now will resume our regularly scheduled programming." The report usually occurred late at night on election day, or in tightly contested races, not until the next day.

It was such a refreshing way to cover an election. It was efficient. It was sensible. Quite simply, it was just plain civilized. People voted, the votes were counted, and the results were reported to the people. Everyone found out what they wanted to know and still got to watch their favorite programs. It was the American Way.

Well, that way has changed. The networks have now decided that just reporting the winners after the votes have been counted is not enough. The goal now is to report the winners in elections *before* all of the votes are counted. And evidently it is quite important to be the first network to make that report. It seems that the networks want to win as much as the candidates.

Being able to project the winners of elections before the votes are counted primarily relies on using information gathered from a technique called exit polling. This technique consists of a lot of media folks standing outside polling places around the country waiting to ask exiting voters how they voted. The secret ballot obviously is a concept that people reporting on elections nowadays do not fully grasp. I think they would prefer that the voting would be done by just a show of hands in front of TV cameras, their network's cameras.

The use of the exit polls to report election results as quickly as possible is the result of living in a society that is dominated by lightning-fast computers and cell phones that allow people to do just about anything they want to do at speeds that would even impress Superman. People want things done now, if not sooner. This phenomenon dictates that anchor people go on the air and say things like, "The polls have just closed in Ohio, and with thirteen votes counted, we are projecting Senator Smedley to be the winner by a landslide."

While making early projections seems to be a rather amazing feat at first glance, it supposedly is relatively easy to do when the exit poll data is examined carefully. For example, in the aforementioned Smedley election, that data showed that Smedley's opponent didn't get the necessary votes from the left-handed, baldheaded, Viagra-using, retired toothpick makers. Evidently that particular group was crucial to the opponent's chances for success. That opponent also needed a good showing from female Puerto Rican doctors, cross-dressing truck drivers, and former professional wrestlers who now teach kindergarten.

Without support from those groups, the opponent's election chances apparently were toast. Smedley carried a greater number than was expected of the members of those constituencies, hence, it was projected he would win in a landslide.

While the exit poll technique supposedly can quickly provide large amounts of data that allows the early projections to be made, the irony is that these early projections still take a very long time to report and analyze. In fact, the reporting and analyzing of the early results is deemed to be so important that the TV coverage now lasts all night long. Consequently, late night talk shows are replaced by political pundits debating why the gay ex-NFL football players who are now United Evangelical Universal Non-Denominational

Free Ministers in Idaho voted the way they did.

Reporting the results is no longer enough; the networks have now decided that we also need to know *why* people voted as they did. Apparently this information explains something about the country that we all need to know as soon as possible.

Today's extensive coverage of elections has pretty much destroyed any chance to see even a little bit of the regularly scheduled programs. Actually, this situation isn't a totally bad thing considering the state of TV programming today. Viewers do need a break from shows like *The Real Housewives of Amish Country* and *America's Got Poets*. The problem is that the respite from these programs on election night is filled with a political coverage that is even more agonizing than the original programming, which is not an easy feat.

The fact of the matter is that the analysis part of election coverage, and I'll try to be tactful here, is tedious, irksome, wearisome, dull, and offensive. The networks need to know that people really aren't interested in such a detailed analysis of why a particular candidate won or lost. And the voters also do not need political pundits to explain what it all means. They just want to know who won.

This attitude of just cut to the chase is also found among the people who don't want fifteen-minute weather reports during the local news shows. What people really want to know is tomorrow's forecast. They already know what happened today and they really don't care why it happened. Just report what will happen tomorrow. Say, "The temperature will be 66 degrees tomorrow and it will not rain," then immediately air the latest edition of *The Bachelor Keeps Up with the Kardashians on the Apprentice During the Great Race*. How simple is that?

Getting back to the elections, one of the most annoying parts of the network coverage is the people who are hired to make those analyses of the elections. More often than not, these folks are retired political types. By "retired," I mean people who lost their last election or people who helped someone else lose their last election. If these experts knew what they were doing, why were they so unsuccessful in their last job? Why should we listen to their expertise? If they knew what they were talking about, wouldn't they still be in office or still helping candidates get elected?

Anyway, election coverage has become burdensome, not to mention time-consuming. There is far too much information available. While I have always believed that a little knowledge is a dangerous thing, I now believe that a lot of knowledge is a disaster. Since there is so much information out there now, far too many people think they need to talk about it all of the time.

When I was a young man, my parents taught me that you shouldn't discuss politics or religion with your friends. Their logic was that such discussions could lead to arguments. I still believe that, and if I refrain from sharing my political beliefs with my friends, I sure as heck will do the same with strangers. If I were ever to be interviewed in one of those exit polls, I would inform the interviewer that how I voted was no one's business. That was my parent's American Way, and it is also mine.

Okay, now to summarize my position on election coverage. Just tell me who won.

And Furthermore, My Fellow Americans...

I have been quite worried lately about my behavior. I even considered going to see a doctor, but then I remembered that my health insurance policy doesn't cover doctor visits. In fact, my policy doesn't allow me to visit a doctor or get within one hundred feet of a nurse. Wait a minute, that "within one hundred feet of a nurse" part isn't in my policy, it's a court order.

Anyway, as it turned out, I really didn't need to see a doctor after all. I closely examined my increasingly bizarre behavior and I was able to diagnose my problem all by myself. (Self-diagnosis is a skill I've developed since having a health insurance policy that doesn't allow me to see a doctor.) Once I knew what my ailment was, I also knew that only time would cure it. You see, I was suffering from an overdose of politics, a little understood but now widespread ailment that has come to be known simply as *politicitis*.

This relatively new ailment exists in part because the communication technologies now being used manage to keep elected officials, and the many political wannabes, in the public eye all of the time, whether we or they want it that way or not. Since there are several twenty-four-hour news networks on television, we are constantly aware of what politicians are doing before they actually do it, while they're doing it, and when they're done.

Add to the extensive TV network coverage the numerous social networks on the Internet, then the politicitis problem is multiplied tenfold. And then there are the millions of folks who go around using their cell phone cameras to take pictures and make videos of political stuff like parades, campaign fundraisers, speeches, and elected officials having a good time at a strip club. The end result is that because of social media like YouTube, Facebook, Twitter, and the innumerable blogs manned by people with far too much time on their hands, everything a politician says or does is served up everywhere all of the time.

This coverage overload is what leads to the occurrence of politicitis. Unfortunately, people who are affected rarely realize that they have it. Since not even Dr. Oz has done a program on the irritation, it is no wonder that people are unaware of the symptoms. I shall correct this problem now by giving people a list of specific behaviors that will make it easier to recognize when one does indeed suffer from the affliction.

SPECIFIC BEHAVIORS OF POLITICITIS

1. Referring to your family and friends as "my volunteers."
2. Decorating your home with balloons and banners.
3. Greeting people at work by shaking their hands and asking for their vote.
4. Challenging your spouse to a series of televised debates about such topics as the correct way to squeeze a tube of toothpaste, the proper position for the toilet lid, and the use of the TV remote.
5. Kissing the babies of people you don't even know.
6. Charging people to have dinner with you and then delivering a speech after dinner in which you outline your positions on everything from deficit reduction to the proper way to load a dishwasher.
7. Having someone drive you around town in a convertible while you sit back in the back seat waving at anyone and everyone.
8. Smiling constantly.
9. Visiting the dentist and then holding a press conference to assure everyone that it was just a routine visit. Then reassuring them your teeth are just fine and you will be able to smile for years to come whether it is necessary or not.

10. Planning to visit poor people so you can tell them how badly you feel about their plight and then canceling the meeting so you can have lunch with rich people.
11. Going around the neighborhood registering people to vote.
12. Telling people who didn't even ask that some of your best friends are gay or black or Hispanic or Indian.
13. Giving a speech in which you attempt to please every human being on the face of the earth.
14. Asking your neighbor to be your press secretary and giving him the responsibility to notify the press whenever you do something meaningful and offering some sort of explanation when you do something stupid.
15. Giving your opinion on every controversial subject known to man, even to people who didn't ask, but only after consulting with 127 advisors for guidance as to what you should think and why.
16. Wearing an American flag pin at all times, even when you are naked.
17. Asking your speechwriter to prepare a speech in which you can easily explain the charges against you for corruption, hiring illegal immigrants, influence peddling, voter fraud, tax evasion, and accepting bribes.

Now if it turns out you are suffering from political overdose, don't panic. Just relax, turn off your TV, computer, and cell phone for two weeks. If this prescription doesn't work, I guess there is the possibility your behavior could help you become the next president of the United States of America. That job at least has a good health insurance plan, one where you actually get to see a doctor.

It's All I'll Know for the Day

It is hard to understand the issues of today,
to know which side to take.
I try to listen to the well-known experts,
so a decision I can make.

But they frequently disagree when making their points,
and that makes me scratch my head.
I shift in my seat, thoughtfully rubbing my chin,
perplexed about what they just said.

They all have facts, which they use quite freely
to explain their many convictions.
But these facts do little to solve their differences,
they only create contradictions.

Shouldn't these experts know all there is to know
about that which they so freely speak?
Shouldn't the pronouncements in their area of expertise
leave the opposition intellectually weak?

But the complexity of any of the oft-debated topics
continues to confound my mind.
No matter how much talking the talking heads do,
my judgment is still purblind.

This situation does produce a quandary for me,
and actually I'm quite disappointed.
After listening to so many celebrated experts,
I'm amazed they ever were anointed.

But while the experts do not live up to their billing,
and I have questions about all that they say,
I still rise each morning to hear their opinions,
cause it's all I'll know for the day.

I'll Have a Burger, Fries and Some Pot

The debate concerning whether or not marijuana should be made legal for recreational as well as medical purposes continues to take place on Willie Nelson's tour bus. Actually, on Willie's bus it is more of a "how-do-we-make-it-happen" strategy discussion, but in many other parts of the country, it is indeed a raging debate. In fact, it has been going on for many, many years.

While those who support the legalization of marijuana have several arguments to support their position, one of their main points is that legalization would bring huge sums of money to the government coffers by having another product that could be subjected to a sin tax.

Some have even proposed that the government should manage marijuana sales much like they currently manage the postal service. That reason, and that reason alone, is why a friend of mine thinks a federal government takeover of the marijuana business would end in disaster.

Actually, it is rather difficult to argue with his logic. Imagine this scene. It unfolds at a government-run marijuana store, Bongs R Us, located at a mall somewhere in the U.S.A. A customer enters the store.

Reefer Man: Hey, man, my friend Crash said I could get weed here. Is that for real?

Bureaucrat: Yes, your friend's information is essentially correct. You can indeed purchase cannabis in this establishment.

Reefer Man: Can-in-a-bus? Dude, I want some weed, grass, pot. I don't know nothin' 'bout can-in-a-bus.

Bureaucrat: Of course you don't. Anyway, we do have many strains of marijuana from which to choose. You do know what marijuana is, don't you?

Reefer Man: Totally, dude. I can dig marijuana. Can I get some here?

Bureaucrat: Sir, this is a marijuana store. We sell marijuana, although we also have some American flags and other patriotic items for sale. It's all part of our plan to lower the national debt. You most certainly can obtain marijuana here and it is all perfectly legal since the passage of H.R. 486936. Do you wish to make a purchase?

Reefer Man: Yo, dude, I told you that already and then you tried to sell me some can-in-a-bus. Man, you are a trip. Just give me a few joints.

Bureaucrat: Wait a minute, before we can make a transaction there is some paperwork to be done.

Reefer Man: Paperwork? What kind of paperwork?

Bureaucrat: Well, there are a few forms that have to be filled out.

Reefer Man: Forms? Dude, when I got my stuff on the street from Loco Louie, he looked down the street, I looked up the street. If we didn't see any cops, he gave me the stuff and I slipped him some bills. Boom. Done deal.

Bureaucrat: Ah, yes, you may have completed the deal with the utmost speed, but that was a most inefficient way to conduct business. We in the federal government pride ourselves in being able to do things in a much more thorough manner. Among other things, our methods allow for greater accuracy in recordkeeping. We are able to know what you buy, when you buy it, and how much you owe, and much more.

Reefer Man: Loco Louie didn't keep records, man. He knew everything that went down in the hood. And he had some big dudes who collected the money. No need for records 'cause none of them dudes could read anyway.

Bureaucrat: But when you made your purchases from this Loco Louie character, you didn't know what you were getting. You could have been buying inferior marijuana or even marijuana that had been sprayed with chemicals. Everything you purchase in this store is USDD choice. It has been inspected and approved for sale by the United States Department of Dope. Trust me, this is a more acceptable way to get your drugs. Now, back to the paperwork.

Reefer Man: Yeah, whatever. Do what you got to do, man.

Bureaucrat: Okay, let's get started. What is your name?

Reefer Man: My friends call me Reefer Man, or sometimes Purple Haze, if I'm really trippin'.

Bureaucrat: Okay, Mr. Man, are you employed?

Reefer Man: Employed? You mean like, do I work? You government folks are some funny dudes. Naw, I'm not really into work. I did try it once and that was enough. Sometimes I do go downtown and watch people work, but it ain't really my thing.

Bureaucrat: How unfortunate. Under the new work incentive program, you could have gotten a discount if you had a job. And if you had mentioned the secret phrase, "I'm looking for a job," I could have given you a small discount. Anyway, moving on. Mr. Man, I'll need to know your address, age, next of kin, last year of school that you finished—

Reefer Man: Yo, dude, stop with the questions. You an ex-game show host or something? I just want some grass, man, I'm not trying to win a car.

Bureaucrat: Mr. Man, I am just trying to do the job the taxpayers pay me to do. You do know what "taxpayers" are, don't you? I suspect not. Anyway, if you would like to register a formal complaint, you can do so by filling out forms ZZX4532 and BS568-6. If your complaint is informal, then of course you just need to fill out form AB11 in triplicate.

Reefer Man: Just chill, man. I ain't complaining about nothing. I just want a couple of joints. I don't need all of this hassle.

Bureaucrat: Hassle? Do you call complying with the law of the land a "hassle"? We are a nation of laws, Mr. Man, and men have gone to war to preserve those laws, to protect your freedoms, one of which now is to purchase good, clean marijuana. You call that a "hassle"?

Reefer Man: Whoa, dude, don't have a cow. You need to puff the dragon, dude, and settle down a bit. Okay, let's get on with these forms.

Bureaucrat: Of course, I'm exceedingly sorry for my outburst. Let us continue. Now, since you have never purchased marijuana from us before, you need to get a physical and take some psychological tests. Then you need to get a security clearance. And if you live in a neighborhood containing anyone under the age of 18, you will have to move. Once you get your marijuana and use it, you will have to report to our quality control department every week.

Reefer Man: Yo, man, I've got to do all of that just to get some pot?

Bureaucrat: Well, you have to first comply with phase one of our three phase program. I'll get to the other two phases in a minute.

Reefer Man: Forget it, man, I'm out of here. I'm off weed, man, I'm going back to booze. Maybe I'll start smoking tofu or something. My girlfriend has been trying to get me on that stuff for a long time. She's a vegetarian pothead. Later, dude.

Bureaucrat: Mr. Man, come back, come back. Acapulco Gold is on sale this week. And we have a "buy two packs of Ganja, get one free special" if you have a coupon.

If those in favor of legalizing marijuana are indeed thinking it will become a cash cow, well, maybe they better think again. Those who want to see marijuana use decline, maybe letting Uncle Sam take over the distribution is the way to go.

CPSIA information can be obtained at www.ICGtesting.com
Printed in the USA
LVOW10s1024040115

421439LV00029B/615/P